Cambrian Dreams

Front cover – 'Shalawi' - an oil painting by Emily Collyer

Printed in Great Britain by
Biddle Books Limited, King's Lynn, Norfolk

Cambrian Dreams

Tales of Riding Across the Welsh Mountains

For Tania Hughes,

All the best!

EJColler

By Emily Collyer

FOREWORD

By Marcus Field

I'm sitting on the back of a pony and I'm terrified. I have ridden before, but never in such extreme conditions. We are trekking up what feels to me like an almost vertical slope, brambles and branches threaten to topple me, and the mud around the pony's feet is so deep and squelchy that the poor animal slips with every step. It's what I imagine riding in the Himalayas would be like, only I'm nine years old so instead of making this romantic comparison I just scream.

"Lean forward and hold onto her neck!" comes a loud command from in front. This is Judith, leader of our small group of intrepid riders. I'm now frightened on two counts; first of having a very undignified and possibly painful fall, and second of being told off for not obeying instructions. So I lean forward, put my arms round the pony's neck, close my eyes, and just cling on for dear life.

This recollection of trekking up the bridle path into Strefford Wood is one of the most vivid memories I have from my many childhood experiences of riding out with Judith Collyer. The pony here was Bonny I think, or possibly Bubbles.

The year was 1976, and I, together with my two sisters, Rosalind and Julia, and my mother, Sue, was spending a week of my summer holidays at Affcot Mill. Sue had been friends with Judith since their school days, and they remained closely bound by their shared memories, as well as by their mischievous sense of humour.

Our week at Affcot Mill became an annual ritual for my family after the Collyers moved to Shropshire from Hertfordshire in 1974.

My father, Ray, would drive us there at the weekend and then return home to work before collecting us the following weekend.

I always looked forward to this visit. We lived in suburbia, so to spend a week in the real countryside, surrounded by goats, chickens, dogs and horses, was an extraordinary adventure for us. I loved the old mill house, with its water pumped from an underground well and its solid fuel Rayburn. Everything about the Collyers' way of life was a novelty for me, and the source of much inspiration too.

At the centre of this magical world was Judith, a strong and capable figure who seemed to take everything in her stride. She could milk goats and wring chickens' necks, as well as keep everybody in line on the many picnic outings we took. On these excursions some of us would ride on horseback, others on bicycles, with any stragglers following behind on foot. Goats and dogs would often come too. Judith could be intimidating for a child, but I quietly admired her impressive country skills and the imaginative life she had made for herself.

These visits now occupy a special place in my memories of childhood, although in reality they perhaps went on for just five or six years. During that time I saw Emily grow up from a new-born baby to fearless rider, always keeping up with the pack on Angus, her equally fearless Shetland pony.

By the early 1980s I had become a surly and confused teenager who didn't much want to spend holidays in the country. We visited Shropshire less, and I stupidly missed my chance to take part in the remarkable treks recorded with such unforgettable detail in this book.

That was my loss. But for my parents and my horse-loving sister, Ros, the treks became a new chapter in our family connection with the Collyers. On several of these adventures they joined Emily and Judith on the journey to the sea, with Sue and Ray driving the luggage and supplies between hostels, and Ros taking part in the daily ride. Sue loved these expeditions and recounted many of the hair-raising episodes on her return.

Years later, she and Judith would talk about turning these stories into a book. Judith promised to write them down, and Sue said she would type them up. Time went on, and other things got in the way.

Now the baton has passed to Emily, and she has done a fantastic job of finally committing these stories to paper. Sadly Sue died in 2017, so she never got to see this book finished. But I know she would have been touched and honoured to see it dedicated in her name.

This book is now a lasting record of those unforgettable journeys across the Welsh mountains. For those who took part I know it will bring back many happy memories. For those who weren't there, it is both a thrilling read and an introduction to that ancient and bewitching landscape that lies between Shropshire and the sea. I hope you enjoy it.

MARCH 2021

Kenchi, Rosie, Sue, Julia and Emily on Angus in front of Affcot Mill in 1981

In Loving Memory of Sue

Sue Field was one of Judy's dearest friends to whom she promised she would write about her treks to the sea.

Judy riding Shally with Sadie following. A sketch by Emily

Welsh Miles

Though the going be tough
And the ground can be rough
The wind can howl, the rain can hail

Yet the air we breathe is sweet and clean
As we climb those hills
For miles upon miles

And the sun can shine
And light up the hills
With gold and purple and space you can feel

We're on top of the world
All Wales is on view
And the sky is our home

With all those Welsh hills
Just rolling around
The river below a silver line

Farmsteads in miniature nestle below
So down to the valley we carefully go
To the tiny people far far below
Welsh miles upon miles

JUDY COLLYER

CONTENTS

INTRODUCTION

This book is about the adventures of a group of horse-loving people during the 80's and 90's. The horse treks from Shropshire to the Welsh coast at the heart of the story were created and led by Judy Collyer, my mother. Over 30 different families took part over the years, starting in 1982 and continuing until 2000. This book puts the adventures we had whilst traversing the Cambrian Mountains, into written memoirs with an array of accompanying photos and route maps.

There is also an abundance of local history to be found in the book associated with the lands ridden through, and sometimes I dip into wider subject matters. From drovers, local characters and uprooted Welsh communities to forts, castles and viaducts, the book is also intended to stir the reader into envisioning life on the old ways in history, as well as the late 20th century.

Leaving the comfort of the homestead tucked under the Wenlock Edge escarpment in South Shropshire, we would weave our way through the Welsh Marches and what was once the historic Kingdom of Mercia when Offa reigned. We cantered beside his dyke before heading on through Powys and the spectacular Radnor Forest ancient hunting ground. Trekking over the Glascwm and Painscastle Hills, we joined old drovers' roads and bridleways along the way.

We climbed up and across Mynydd Epynt firing range with its military presence, bullets clinking beneath our horses' hooves amidst the booming of explosives.

Journeying on through the Welsh spa towns we then traversed the vast upland plateau known as the Elenydd, staying in remote hostels with no electricity and sometimes no running water. In these places our horses roamed freely on the mountains at night.

Finally, we threaded our way over the Dyfed coastal headland and came upon the sea at Llangrannog.

The Cambrian Dream became a rooted tradition stretching over 14 years. Upon the school bell of the summer holidays, the horses were saddled and the routes that were planned during the cold winter months in front of the fire with a map were ventured. The final destination may have been the same, but each trek was unique.

You will hear tales of treacherous mires, wild stallions, rearing horses, precipitous cliff edges and a farmer with a shotgun. You will hear about the Devil himself.

Often bedding down in the most basic accommodation, we shared a journey where money and status had no place or importance. Where mobile phones were thankfully still rare and phone signal even rarer. There were happy, sad, funny and terrifying moments. There were ups and downs both with the lay of the land and with rudimentary human emotions and spirits.

Many of the folk who trekked with Judy share comments such as "It made me tough", "It was character building", "It gave me resilience" and "It's still up there as one of my best childhood memories".

I certainly share my mother's sense of adventure and have foot-raced through the Alps, completed fell races and ultra marathons. Always feeling drawn to wild and wondrous places, I avoid queues and crowds like they are the plague. Now I take my kids on cycle treks, I'd say a little tamer than my childhood adventures, but adventures all the same. I think the physical toughness that grew within me from those treks and being raised on a smallholding no doubt set me up for my 17 years as a firefighter.

The book is divided into two sections; the first explores Judy's early horse orientated years in Hertfordshire, followed by our family's settlement in Shropshire. Talking a little about life as a child on the smallholding, I also mention the various treks that Judy organised aside from the journeys to Llangrannog.

The second part of the book is dedicated to the many years of trekking from Affcot Mill to Llangrannog.

Finally the appendices provide extra information on various aspects of the adventures and finish with an account Judith wrote in 2006 about time spent with her last horse before putting her saddle away and focussing on her chickens, cats and dogs.

It is my hope that this book will be of interest to any horse-lover, countryside lover, traveller, adventurer and those with an interest in mid-Welsh local history in addition to the many people who took part in the treks.

Local information about the history of various places was taken from the books and websites cited in the bibliography. Although hopefully accurate to a degree, this book is not meant to be a factual encyclopaedia and apologies are given for any inaccuracies printed.

Having tried my best to locate and contact all the people who took part in the treks in any capacity, riding or crewing, I hope those whom I've been unable to find, will understand.

I have sought permission to use the photos in the manuscript wherever possible and if I've missed any permissions then I apologise. Many of the photos are my own.

The maps found within the book focus on the established route used during the later years of trekking, although there were many variations used over the years. The maps created by me are of a fantasy nature and are not accurate or to scale with respect to boundaries or any other parameters.

PART I

SETTLING IN SHROPSHIRE

CHAPTER I

Dreams... Once Upon A Horse

"My childhood dreams.... To have a pony of my
own.... To ride that pony to the sea"

JUDY COLLYER

When Judy's parents - Norman and Mary Clare - agreed that Judith could have a pony if she saved her pocket money, they never expected her to achieve her ambition.

In 1954 when Judy turned 14 years old, and after selling her handmade cane table mats to the John Lewis department store, she'd saved enough money to buy Chalice.

Chalice came on a train from Lincolnshire to Stevenage. Judy bred her with "Turton Story" in Hertfordshire and Chalice had two foals, Shane and Tina.

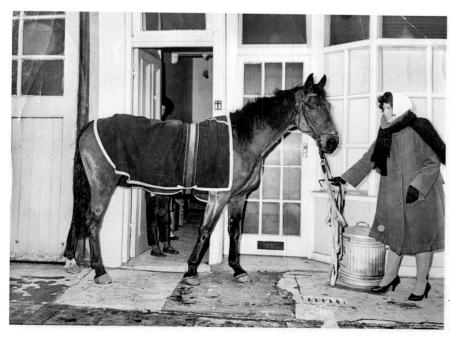

Judy with Chalice
in Hertfordshire
approx 1959

*Judy on Chalice
in Hertfordshire
approx 1957*

*Judy with Chalice's
first-born Shane,
as a foal in
Hertfordshire
approx 1959*

In 1974 Judy moved to Shropshire with her family, my father Ted, myself and my two brothers, Paul and Oliver, bringing Tina and Shane with her. Eight years later she realised her second dream, when she rode across the Welsh hills on Tina to the sea.

Judy and Ted set about creating a small holding at Affcot Mill where over the years the menagerie included horses, ponies, goats, sheep,

Judy with Chalice and her foal, Shane in approx 1959

cows, geese, ducks, chickens, rabbits, cats and dogs. In his retirement my father built stables, sheds and created a vegetable garden, later dedicating more and more time to his oil paintings. Our family grew to seven in 1980 when my parents adopted my younger siblings, Rosie and Kenchi. The "Good Life" continued for Judy as she took all her children to pony club events ranging from camps, rallies to fancy dress events. Then show jumping, hunter trials, mounted games and one-day events as we grew older. I recently found a rosette awarded to Judy for taking 37 children to Pony Club rallies in a single year.

I never doubt that I was very privileged to grow up in such a beautiful place surrounded by ponies, however excuse my language when I say it was bloody tough physically. The memories of our traditional "Sunday Rides" may bring shivers to my siblings' spines. Judy started the endurance riding with us very young and we rode for many hours, often on freezing and wet, cold winter days. Toes and fingers numb, icy hazel twigs whipping at our faces, weaving along Wenlock Edge as night time began to envelop the forest and the owls began to hoot. It was incredibly physically demanding, and I'd be lying if I said I didn't frequently wish to be at home with dad in the warmth of the kitchen, helping him make our Sunday roast.

The sticky clay soil that coats the land at Affcot Mill meant the ponies had to be stabled during the winter as the field would get too churned up and grass growth would be hampered the following spring. The stabling meant that the ponies needed to be exercised every day all through the winter.

We all knew that the cold walk home after school from the bus stop wouldn't be followed by getting warm and snug in front of the fire watching "Home and Away" like we yearned, but rather a brisk trot around the lanes followed by the daily mucking out and mixing of feeds. Sometimes, perhaps because I was the keenest of the five children, I would exercise two or three ponies after school and muck out the same number. This leads me onto my ingrained "muck-heap envy". Rather than tipping the horse poo and straw onto a big pile to rot down and be spread on the fields with a tractor and spreader later in the year, like all the other horse owners we knew, every nugget of horse manure and bedding removed from the six earthen-floored stables had to be put into a wheel barrow and pushed up the steep field and spread around with a pitch fork. It was easier in the frost because our wellies wouldn't slip landing us face-first into the barrow of horse poo. The slipping happened many times. I once managed to stab my own palm with a shitty pitch fork at the top of that field. I've still no idea quite how it happened.

The same mucking out was required of the cow shed, only that was a job for the summer as the Dexter cows kept warm with deep litter in the winter. The problem with the summer mucking out was that the manure had dried rock-hard and to get it into a barrow, you had to literally jump on top of the spade and "slice" pieces of cow poo for your awaiting barrow. Therefore we also earned our roast beef.

The view out across Apedale to the Longmynd however has always been wonderful. The villages of Strefford and Wistanstow can be seen nestled in the valley, with rooftops and a church spire poking out above the trees. With the empty barrow waiting and the hard work done, I would often gaze at the traffic trundling along the A49 and the trains rolling past in the distance whilst sat upon the tyre swing that still dangles from the bough of the 300 year old oak tree. The cantering around and jumping on the horses bareback during the long balmy summer evenings made up for the hard winter graft in my eyes. The feeling of cantering along narrow twisting paths in the woodlands was akin to a roller coaster at times. The dappled sunlight would glitter in the forest as Lassie and I raced against my siblings and their ponies. The hours spent grooming and caring for the ponies were often blissful hours, kissing the soft velvet of their muzzles and brushing their coats to a silky sheen. The rugs wrapped around their silky clipped coats which glistened beneath the warm cobweb laced stable lights. Meticulously detangling and oiling a cascading long tail is all part of the wonderful therapy that horses can bestow.

The summer days also had their fair share of hard graft. The baling season brought with it long days of scratched legs and sore palms from collecting hundreds of bales of hay straight from the farmers' fields and ramming them into the Tardis that was our horse trailer. The hay was always cheaper if collected from the fields rather than delivered and with her five child strong work force bundled into the back of the Land Rover Judith took full advantage of the discount. The hay fields were fun however as we climbed on top of the stacks to push the bales off, jumping down after them and chasing the Land Rover with its rattling trailer, ramp dragging along the short dry grass to the next stack.

How tired I used to feel when we got home after each journey and stacked the barns to the brim with the bales that were to be stored for the following winter. Endless bales were rolled, lifted and hoisted during hot summer evenings wearing our shorts and vests. The combination of sun burn and hay scratches made for painful baths after the days' work.

Over the years there were various nanny goats on the smallholding. Heidi, Grizelda, Easter and Lavinia provided us with fresh milk which we all despised unless it was disguised as cow's milk in a commercial cow's milk bottle, in which case we drank it quite happily.

There were often baby goats around in order to keep Grizelda and Co's milk flowing, and the nannies were always easily sold. The billy goats however, who couldn't be sold, went into the freezer as goats only to come back out as "lamb" in a bid for the family to eat them. I knew it was goat meat. I didn't care but I think the others felt differently.

I learnt fairly young not to name the cute orphan lambs that I bottle-fed. I also used to help mother put a band around their tails and testes using an awful metal contraption. I would watch them walk off like John Wayne whilst mother assured me it didn't hurt them. The roast lamb tasted good though, as did the roast chicken, goose and duck.

The following excerpt is from a journal Judy wrote following the 1989 trek to the coast, and other excerpts from the same piece crop up throughout the book.

"Shropshire had always been in my imagination since I had read the Lone Pine 5 books by Malcolm Saville as a teenager in Hertfordshire.

I used to imagine myself riding my horse on the Longmynd, both up and down its steep gullies and along its ridge, flying across to view the Devil's Chair on the Stiperstones, where my trusty steed with flowing mane and tail would turn and take me back to safety before the mist shrouded the rocks and "HE" was there. "HE" being the Devil who sits in his chair when the mist comes down."

Judy with her two boys, Paul and Oliver, sitting upon Shane in Shropshire. Tina is grazing in the background. 1974

Tina with her first-born, "Shropshire Lad", in 1974. Shropshire Lad later sired Shropshire Lass (Lassie) who became my trekking pony. Lassie also had a foal of her own who also trekked to the sea.

Tina had another foal later, a beautiful palomino called Janie, who had an Arabian sire; Corve Golden Showers. Janie trekked to the sea many times, as did her son Mandela. The above photo is of Janie and I at Kyre Hunter Trials in the 80's. Included in the back of the book is a horse family tree, showing the descendants of Judy's childhood pony, Chalice

Either side of Judy's second dream, in which she rode Tina to the sea, she organised and led a number of shorter treks through Shropshire and Powys and she sometimes took United Pack Pony Club Members with her. Judy continues :

"When my various children were able to ride ponies – usually before they could walk and very soon after they sat up - we went on our first ever trek. This was to Wilderhope Manor youth hostel and back again the next day. A habit had begun….

I took various pony club children on treks over the Shropshire and Welsh hills. My Emily was only 5 years old when we went to Wilderhope, Bridges and Clun youth hostels. Then we ventured as far as Knighton and Glascwm youth hostels. Glascwm nestles in the mountains around Builth Wells. On another trek with the Pony Club we went across and along the Longmynd, through Plowden Woods to Lydbury North and Lower Down to Clun."

Amidst the herd of horses and ponies bred by Judy there were other ponies that came to live at Affcot Mill. Perhaps most notable to all who knew the family was Angus. Angus was a 10hh Shetland gelding bought for me on my 5th birthday when he was aged just two. My father built a wonderful Shetland pony sized stable which happened to be heated by the kitchen Rayburn pipe on the back of the Mill. Mother brought Angus home in the back of her Land Rover Series II and clearly remembers the warm feeling as he crapped down her collar whilst she was driving.

Angus and I learned together. He would buck me off every single day during our early years and I would determinedly get back on crying with frustration rather than pain. Angus also used to take a dislike to certain people, often lads. He would chase Marcus and Richard, the sons of our visiting friends, with a glint in his eye that saw them run to the nearest gate and bail over. It was never advised to mock Angus in any way, his size was no reflection of his personality. He never trekked to the sea although he did local treks, which were certainly far enough for his little legs.

Angus and me in 1979

I was just five and riding Angus when I used to get left behind and frightened by a character called Bill from Clun known as "Dummy Lock". He would scream right next to me. I remember looking at his taped up walking stick in fear as I saw the ponies ahead getting further and further away. Angus used to make his own mind up about when to suddenly bolt to catch up. Bill was deaf and dumb but was actually very fond of horses and children, which no doubt was the reason he liked to walk beside Angus and me. His shrieks and screams were well known and believed to be his way of releasing frustrations. I was utterly terrified. I will talk more about Bill Lock later in the book when we look at the local history of South Shropshire and specifically Clun.

Waiting to start a local trek from Strefford with United Pack Pony Club members 1984

Shropshire Lass (Lassie) was my Welsh Mountain Thoroughbred cross and great granddaughter to Chalice. She had a foal of her own in the years to follow. Her half-sister Bronwen "Mugger" is to the left. She gets up to mischief at Clun YHA later in the story (1984)

SHROPSHIRE STAR THURSDAY AUGUST 28, 1980 5

Four-day trek by the pony club riders

A party of young riders from the United Pack Pony Club are taking part in a four-day trek in South Shropshire.

The 15 youngsters and three adults set off from Strefford Ford, near Craven Arms, on Monday on the first stage of the ride across Wenlock Edge to Wilderhope Manor.

The next stage in the 45-mile trip will take them to the Bridges, near Ratlinghope, and on to Clun before returning to Craven Arms. They will spend each night in a youth hostel.

The trek leaders are Mrs Judy Collyer, Mrs Joyce Machin and Mrs Sue Truman.

Trek leaders are (left), Mrs Judy Collyer, Becky Trueman, Mrs Joy Brightman and Emily Collyer. More pictures on Monday.

Pictured above in the Shropshire Star, Thursday August 28th, 1980 are Judy, Beck, Joy Brightman and myself. Joy was our very efficient pony club DC and used to visit the hostels in the evening to do a 'tack inspection'. This wasn't the norm on Judy's treks at all and I remember being told by mother to "pretend" to be cleaning my bridle until she'd left. Generally, the biggest clods would get brushed off the tack as we set off the next morning and a more thorough job carried out after we had finished our adventure

In the Spring of 1990, tucked in between the many treks to Llangrannog, was an odyssey through the Black Mountains via Hay-On-Wye. Away on a Pony Club exchange in the USA I was not part of this particular adventure. A combination of Russells, Truemans, Hays, Collyers, Machins and a Wheeler rode their horses south through the Welsh Marches staying at Knighton and Glascwm, before trekking south to Painscastle and picking up some bridleways on the Begwyns. They then rode along country lanes to Clyro and into the beautiful Wye Valley where they rode through the centre of Hay–on–Wye, crossing the vast river over the town's grand bridge.

It was at Glascwm youth hostel that Celia spent her birthday that year. Celebrations were had and her husband arrived with a gift. As she unravelled the wrapping paper Barry declared "I can see you in that my love!" A somewhat confused look spread over Celia's face. "Why have you wrapped up my outfit from my wardrobe at home dear?" she asked. It slowly became clear that he had in fact already "Seen her in that" as she'd previously bought it and WORN it out with him. It caused much amusement and the story lives on when I chat to the trekkers today. Robbie reminds me that Barry had quite correctly kept the receipt for the duplicate outfit he had bought but when he took it back it had been reduced and he was only reimbursed with the sale price.

Untacking after a long days riding from Knighton in Spring 1990. The trekkers were bound for Hay on Wye and the Black Mountains the following day. James making a fuss of Jess the retriever and Rosie unsaddling Maz outside Glascwm youth hostel

The riders cross the river at Hay-On-Wye in the Spring of 1990 on their way to the Black Mountains and Capel y Ffin YHA

14

Joyce and Tim riding Peggy and Troy under the shade of the trees outside Glascwm hostel 1990

After the town they climbed to the west of the great summit that is Hay Bluff which itself straddles the border. Most of the mountain is in Powys yet parts of its eastern flanks lie in the English county of Herefordshire. Close to Offa's Dyke they took an open lane called Gospel Pass; the highest road pass in Wales reaching 549 metres above sea level. The open lane is squeezed between Twmpa mountain and Hay Bluff and leads to a youth hostel known as Capel y Ffin before heading on to Llanthony Priory.

My sister Rosie recalls seeing many hang gliders launching themselves from the top of the steep scarp, it must have been quite a sight to see and quite a surprise for the young, green horses in the herd.

The hostel which the trekkers bedded down in was a former farmhouse which opened as a hostel in 1958 and continued to provide accommodation for travellers until 2007. The horses were accommodated at the local trekking centre and some of the dads and husbands stayed in the hotel at the spectacular Llanthony Priory. The route was an "out and back" venture with a day's rest at the hostel nestled in the spectacular Black Mountain massif.

Rob was crewing for the trekkers that year when Bob Trueman, one of the riders, had to rush off to London for a business meeting. With it being a little too far to ride to London, he took Rob's Daihatsu and left Rob car-less. Rob thought a few beers in the Llanthony Priory might now be acceptable, by all accounts perhaps a few too many were had. However Bob had left his horse "Chester" with the trekkers and, as Robbie was not a keen rider, Sue led Chester all the way back to Shropshire from her horse, which was three days of trekking.

Crossing land through Wales and England on routes that may not have been regularly used always had potential for arguments. Recollections of angry farmers were prevalent as I talked to the 70 or so people who trekked with Judy over the years

The public bridleways enthusiastically marked with arrows onto a map in front of the cosy fire in the Winter months at Affcot Mill were often a far cry from what lay before us in the wild countryside exposed to the elements.

On our treks we regularly encountered padlocks, barbed wire, farm machinery and electric fences put up by landowners. Meanwhile Mother Nature herself presented us with brambles, nettles, midges, horse flies, hot sun, floods, storms and treacherous bogs. It became second nature to head for the tail end of a gate and wrestle it off its hinges when the opening end was impossible. This was easier than undoing a metre of rusty barbed wire that had often been coiled around the gate post, burying the gate bar within.

There were many lost and cast shoes over the years, and soreness from the barefoot ponies. Lassie never wore a shoe; not once had a nail been driven through her little black hooves to secure the iron. Her feet themselves were as hard as nails and she never got sore. Farriers were called upon various times for other ponies as we made our way deeper into the heart of Wales.

Whilst Judy always tried to stick to the rights of way, when she had to deviate so did the other 15 or so horses and riders and accompanying dogs. There was drama… often… especially in the early years before a good passable route had been established.

One such drama happened en-route to Ynyslas in 1982. On this occasion Judy resorted to whipping a farmer with her crop when he grabbed the reins of Kerry's head-shy horse Sorrell, who tried to rear up. "Cool it lady! Cool it!" the man yelled as he released his grasp and backed away.

Mother never failed to vehemently stand her ground and get us all through so we could get to our hostel beds each night. There were always a lot of children with us and it was rarely an option to retrace our steps miles to find another route that wasn't blocked. Although I remember being scared of furious farmers, we were (nearly) always in the right and the map was hung as evidence around Judy's neck at all times.

Several trekkers have reminded me about the incident where we were threatened by a farmer with a shotgun. He fired it into the air. With this being a lot closer to home than you may imagine, perhaps somethings are best left in the past.

Those 'not so friendly' folk were the exception of course, and there were countless friendly faces and well-wishers on our journeys.

Other events remain a mystery, such as where we might have been when we wandered into a great quarry at the end of one day. Monster construction vehicles were parked motionless in a line; although silent they were still freakish enough to frighten the herd, with their great tyres as high as the horses' withers. Tired and lost, we were placed unexpectedly into a hard grey-steel world, far from the green soft landscapes we had become accustomed to. Rich chestnuts, bays and Palominos must have brightened the image of that quarry for those uncomfortable minutes before we left, returning it back to its monochrome expanse.

Never phased by the challenges, again and again Judy took her equine tribe across the Cambrian Mountains, improving the route and adding to the plethora of tales.

The Llangrannog treks continued for 14 years from 1986 to 2000 with the route being tweaked due to a myriad of reasons such as access, accommodation and topography. It became a summer holiday tradition. Over 70 people joined in at one point or another, and Judy continued to lead the treks well after the Collyer children had flown the nest. I'm happy to say I was a part of the last trek to Llangrannog

Judy in 1999 upon Mandela, great-grandson of Chalice

in 2000 after being away from the trekking scene for a few years.

Then in 2001 Foot and Mouth struck the UK and cross country travel was forbidden in an effort to prevent the spread of disease.

At the end of the 2001 summer, Judy managed to organise a short trek along the Jack Mytton Way which had by that point reopened. Judy, Jan, Sue, Charlie and Helen rode Zac, Dusty, Rijal and Mandela with our golden retrievers, Holly and Cassie, running behind. They rode 18 forested miles along Wenlock Edge to Stokes Barn at Much Wenlock where they stayed. Judy writes about a section of their ride that day:

> *"Because so few people had ridden all Spring and Summer (due to Foot and Mouth restrictions) the vegetation knew no bounds and our track petered out… Dusty did not like being amongst branches and brambles as our track disappeared. He did some bucks amidst the jungle, which alarmed poor Helen. However my instincts proved right and after some difficult climbing over roots and brambles and under branches we came back onto the main track above us. Phew!"*

They then meandered along Shropshire bridleways and lanes to The Croft at Morville where they bedded down for the night. The third day saw them riding near the Severn Valley to Billingsley Hall Farm where they enjoyed "tea, hot baths and a log fire" after a rainy day in their saddles.

The fourth and final day of riding was a long 28 miles, bringing them home after heading westward to Brown Clee Hill, across the Corvedale to Millichope, back onto Wenlock Edge and down through the woods to Affcot.

By 2001 Judy's Appaloosa, Zacharia, was competing and placing well in endurance competitions and this became her focus. Judy took him, his rider Ursula, and their crew who included Charlotte, to compete as part of the British Intermediate Team in Compiegne in France in 2003. The focus had by then shifted away from the Llangrannog treks and I think although she aspired to trek abroad, Judy's grand children came along thick and fast and priorities changed.

The Jack Mytton Way trek in September 2001, arranged when local bridle ways were finally reopened after the Foot and Mouth outbreak. Charlie, Jan, Helen and Judy in the pink shirt on her Apoloosa horse Zac

The following chapter tells the tale of the journey to Ynyslas. Part II of the book will then focus on the memories made during the many yearly treks to Llangrannog.

CHAPTER 2
Distant Sands of Ynyslas

It was 1982, and I was just 8 when my mother first led us to the coast on horseback. Three families took part, Collyers, Machins and Haynes, and we trekked to Ynyslas near Borth from Affcot Mill.

I have vague recollections of that particular trek, but most of this book will focus on the many treks to the wonderful town of Llangrannog. Not to say that the journey across mid Wales on a more northerly line was not as adventurous. It was just not repeated by us. In Judy's words…

> *"We became more adventurous and decided to 'trek to the sea'. Borth, just a three mile gallop along the sands from Aberystwyth, was our destination. That took five days riding, a week playing in the sea with the horses, and five days trekking back"*

For many of the riders who trekked from Shropshire with Judy in 1982, it was their first experience of riding horses in the sea. And what an experience that is, especially if you can persuade your horse to go deep.

My Lassie did, just like all the other horses and ponies that were bred from Chalice, as if it were in their blood. The feeling of a horse swimming under you is incredible. You really have to hang on to their manes as their swimming action can be like a fairground ride, lunging as their hind feet push up off the sand banks until they swim out of their depth and it becomes a little gentler. We would be bareback as the tack was usually leather and the saltwater would damage it. Bareback in swimming costumes, holding on for our lives.

From Affcot, the first part of the route we rode on this trek is not clear in our memories. Looking at old, marked maps it seems likely that we went to Clun, then across the hills to Beguildy, staying at a B&B and then on to Nant Y Dernol YHA. Judy remembers riding along the Kerry Ridgeway; we may have headed up towards the Anchor from Clun to join the ancient ridgeway and then dropped southerly via a B&B to pick up the marked route, crossing the Wye at Dolhelfa and on to Nant Y Dernol youth hostel.

We crossed many bogs and mires on those Cambrian "Bridleways" that year; I vividly recall Pal, a 16hh Palomino hunter type who Tania rode, sinking to his belly. After an initial flounder where Tania jumped off, he quietly waited to gather energy to make his bid for freedom. Tania was kneeling next to him sobbing and embracing his neck, calling for her mother Joyce, who was with her new baby in arms, far away.

Thankfully Tania was too light to break the surface of the bog herself. Pal did manage to drag his hind legs from the sucking black treacle and we all lived to tell the tale although when I read "Harquin – The Fox That went Down to The Valley" to my children now, as Harquin leads the hunt through the bogs and the horses and riders go down, it perhaps has a little more impact on me than other parents who laugh at such comedy.

Nant Y Dernol, Tan-yr-Allt closed in 1987. It was a small, simple hostel and was previously an old shepherd's hut, three up, two down and was built sometime in the 19th century. According to the YHA archive catalogue, the building was still standing in 2011. It is pictured below.

YOUTH HOSTEL, NANT-Y-DERNOL, LLANGURIG, MONTGOMERYSHIRE

Photo : R.T.Russell

From here we rode on to Blaenycwm and Cwmystwyth towards Devil's Bridge and Ystumtuen YHA. There are not many bridleways shown on the old map, so we must have ridden on a lot of tarmac between these two hostels.

If memories and accounts of this trek by the three families who took part are mostly faded and patchy, then the united recollection of what happened at Devil's Bridge only emphasizes its impact. We arrived at Devil's Bridge, by now with both horses and riders exhausted and seeking a welcome break before the final push to the youth hostel.

Below is the picture of the lay-by opposite the hotel where we gathered with ours horses.

View from Hotel, Devil's Bridge.   WT.396R

An old postcard of the view from the hotel at Devil's Bridge

The lay-by is where many of our tired steeds decided to immediately crap. This was to the fury of the hotel owner who demanded we take our horses and leave. There was shouting and cursing as Judy and Maurice defended our position. I recall the hotel keeper grasping Maurice by the throat against the wall above the canyon.

"You see that picture hanging up there!?" My mother screamed at the angry landlord whilst pointing to the pub sign bearing the devil himself. "Yes, that's me!" he hollered back at her. "Yes, it's you!" she affirmed.

I'm not clear whether this was one of the times mother got out her riding crop as a weapon, but the angry man managed to get hold of Belinda's whip (I can only assume in self-defence) and, perhaps then thinking better of challenging mother to a duel, launched it over the wall into the abyss. The whole affair was extremely terrifying, although it seems hilarious now, re-telling the story nearly forty years on. It's often crossed my mind that one of the reasons I may be writing this book, is for closure.

So on to Ystumtuen we went with adrenaline pumping and the horses feeling a little lighter!

We collected many of the fabric badges from the Youth Hostels from our travels, most of them are now faded and moth eaten. John Martin, the YHA archivist, has kindly provided images of some in his collection and, like the one below, they can be found scattered throughout the book.

Ystumtuen YHA, a former school used as a hostel from 1960-1999

On the final day we rode to Borth and on to Ynyslas, where we met my father and younger brother and sister, Kenchi and Rosie. On the morning of that last day however, Belinda's pony – Dinky, had become lame and it was decided he should be left at the hostel. Chris decided to lead her daughter, Belinda on her own horse Amy, whilst she walked along by her side.

Soon however, they became separated from the rest of the trekkers and although Tania was sent back to find them, they never managed to reunite. To Chris's horror she walked 20 long miles across the hills with Belinda aged 9. No water, no compass or map. Miraculously they managed to find their way off the mountains on the correct track and down to Borth. It was a harrowing affair for Chris and Belinda, and I'm sure for Maurice too when the other riders turned up without his wife and daughter. All was well in the end but a lesson had been learned about staying together at all times in the future. A group left behind only need take one different fork in a track and before long they are in a different valley heading in a completely different direction and anybody sent back to find them clearly wouldn't.

Beside the sea at Ynyslas we stayed in a static caravan and the horses grazed on the salt marshes for a week before we rode all the way back home.

The teenagers on that trek now laugh about young love. One of our lads fell in love with one of our lasses on the first day and the others heard nothing else for the whole journey. I won't mention names, but my brother remembers going to watch Grease at the caravan park in a group. I'd have been tucked up in bed by then.

I can recall galloping along that long beach on Lassie and jumping the breakwater boards. They were perfect as you could choose what height to jump, lower towards the sea and higher towards the sand dunes. Lassie and I used to excel at Chase-Me-Charlie which is the Pony Club version of "The Wall "on Horse of the Year Show, where they keep raising the wall and the highest jumper wins. Lassie and I had a lot of fun practicing on that beach. It was quite a shock to us when we cleared a family having a picnic who were sheltered behind one of the breakwater boards. There was shock all around as the family gazed up at a bay tummy and flying hooves, and all the riders had a quick look the other side before jumping thereafter.

FRIDAY SEPTEMBER 12TH 1982   CAMBRIAN NEWS   PAGE 12

Family trek — for horses and riders

The Mayor of Borth, Cllr. Aran Morris, and the long-distance riders.

HAVING always fancied riding to the seaside (well everybody uses cars) members of three families from Church Stretton in Shropshire decided that this was the year to embark on their ambitiion and join the rest of their families on holiday at Ty Gwyn Farm, Ynyslas, where they were camping.

Ten riders from the age of eight upwards set off on the trek across country using bridlepaths and coming right along the top of the mountains for five days and four nights.

Judy Collier led the way on her home-bred thoroughbred dark brown mare, 21-year-old Tina, to coplete the 'family trek' was Tina's four-year-old grand-daughter, Lassie. In contrast to the thoroughbreds were tiny, tough little Welsh mountain ponies, a palomino, an appaloosa, cobs and some enchanting little mountain and moorland types.

During their stay the ponies enjoyed the salted meadows of Ty Gwyn Farm, Ynyslas, and were always ready to be taken to the beach where they spent many hours swimming in the sea.

On Thursday morning they were saddled up to go to the beach for their last canter. They were wished well on their long treck home by the Mayor, Councillor Aran Morris and the Deputy Mayor and owner of Ty Gwyn Farm, Councillor Ber-

wyn Lewis.

Judy Collier says they thoroughly enjoyed their ride to and stay in Ynyslas and have enjoyed wonderful hospitality throughout their journey. "We will be back next year", says Judy. "We certainly hope so—if there is always a welcome in the hillside there is certainly a welcome for such a plucky team in Borth at the Seaside".

Will

Mr. David William EVANS, Gorsfawr, Bronant, who die on May 2nd last, intestate, le estate valued at £43,144 gro £40,556 net. Letters of Adm nistration have been granted Mrs. Betty A. Evans, and M Margaret Powell, of Dolgarro Maesfelin, Llanrhystud.

The Mayor of Borth saw us start our trek home in 1982 as the article from the Cambrian News above shows

Sea horses at Ynyslas, 1982.

Tania riding Pal in the foreground, 1982. Bareback in the sea became the norm so as not to expose the leather saddles to salt water.

There ends our first adventure trekking to the sea and an addiction had started.

Judy writes:

> *"But I was not impressed with Borth as a place to stay, although the route across the mountains to get there was magnificent. No, I prefer my seaside to be cliffs, coves, rocks, caves and peninsulas, not vast stretches of sand. I was used to Cornwall, but we could hardly ride there in five days. Sue Truman told me about Llangrannog in Cardigan Bay, where she spent her childhood. It sounded just my cup of tea, so we planned a trek there."*

At this point I hope I have coloured in some of the background, thereby setting the scene from which I will take you... from Affcot Mill to Llangrannog, 126 miles on horseback...

PART II

SHROPSHIRE TO LLANGRANNOG

Image showing the route to Ynslas and two variations of the Llangrannog treks.
The middle route became our favourite, an established and reasonably safe choice

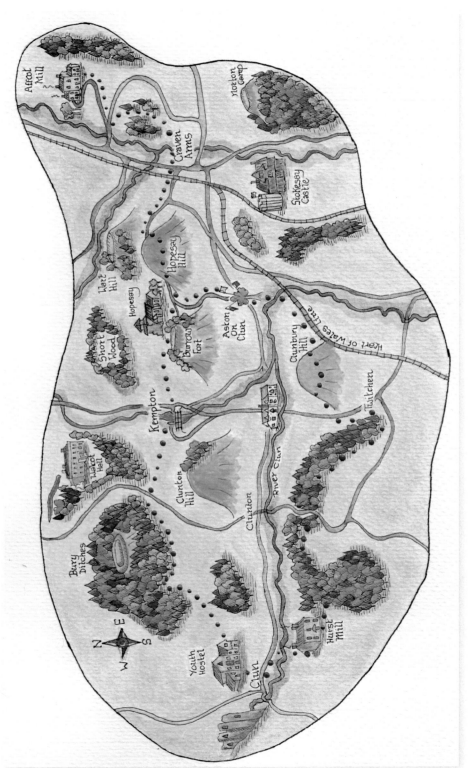

Day 1 – Affcot Mill to Clun Mill. Showing some of the different routes taken over the years. Note the abundance of hill forts

Chapter 3

Mill to Mill

On the first trek to Llangrannog in 1986 we were armed with wire cutters, hand saws and knives to help us negotiate blocked bridleways. These were packed after reflecting on our previous experiences. Our saddlebags were filled to overflowing with our essentials for a six day journey.

These were the days before we had a back-up crew consisting of a Land Rover, a driver and a passenger who would meet us with lunch and then again in the evenings with all our things for the overnight stay. In the early days we carried our overnight items with us. Each horse or pony had a set of saddlebags proportional to its size. Sometimes if the saddles were not perfectly fitted or the bags too heavy, saddle sores appeared. We would then ride bare-back to let them heal until we reached the beach, where if we could persuade the horse to swim, the salt water would wash over their back and help to heal the rubs more quickly.

Ruth remembers us turning up at our destination one evening and frantically looking for a field to put the horses in as well as some concentrate feed to replenish their energy. The early treks were certainly a steep learning curve and the treks became more organised with time.

I vividly remember mother telling me to pack one pair of comfy trousers for the hostels. In went my favourite pink and white striped leggings, and they felt truly heavenly at the hostels after peeling off (probably rain soaked) jodhpurs and boots and pulling on these soft leggings and espadrilles.

We also had to take our own "sheet sleeping bags" to use at hostels. In the days before sheets and pillowcases were freshly laundered for hostellers, we would tuck the pillows into the slip and wriggle into the sleeping bag with multiple blankets strewn over the top. There were no duvets then, and quite often the hostels were heated with a log fire.

Some places didn't even have electricity and lighting was by means of paraffin lamps. There was a minimal yet homely feel that drew travellers together, all on their own adventures.

There were also duties for each hosteller to carry out on a rota system. Cleaning, sweeping and basic housekeeping. Everybody contributed some of their time, together with a warden who often lived on site or nearby.

Day one from Affcot Mill to Clun Mill YHA was a 12 mile ride providing there were no wrong turns which happened every so often. We were set to ride through the marches, the border lands between England and Wales and areas where many hills are topped with forts, a testament to their turbulent history.

This corner of Shropshire has long been fought over. William the Conqueror was England's first Norman king, reigning from 1066 until 1087. Anxious to stabilise his boundaries, he offered some of his knights the opportunity to acquire lands for themselves. Whatever they were able to win from the Welsh princes they were to govern as almost independent kingdoms. These became the marches and were an important feature of border territory. A virtual wall of castles was built to protect it.

Slightly east of the marches, tucked under Wenlock Edge where the Byne and the Quinny brooks meet, is Affcot Mill. A Grade II listed building in the parish of Wistanstow, it was once a corn mill powered

The 18 mile scarp of Wenlock Edge. A copy from an old postcard. Affcot Mill is located just above the red dot

by a water wheel. Built in the late 18th century with sandstone rubble, it was later divided into three houses after a period being the laundry house for the Grove Estate. My parents bought the large central and righthand parts of it in 1974, and it remains our family home.

Affcot Mill

Saddled up and excited, we would begin each trek from the Mill along the lanes, woodland paths and fields to Halford. Only once do I remember the heavens opening as we trotted along the lane, saturated within the first mile. At least it was "warm summer rain", Judy's words would echo back to us amidst the clip clop of hooves. Ever the optimist.

After the rain there was sunshine and euphoria filling the Shropshire air, and the horses were fresh and lively. I used to help plan and pack for weeks beforehand, writing our lists and meticulously crossing items off as they were either jammed into already full saddle bags, or packed into the trusty Land Rover that would be driven, pushed or rolled dutifully by the designated person each day.

I'm sure my father used to breathe a huge sigh of relief as his wife and five kids disappeared out of sight for 6 weeks with a swish of the last pony's tail. I wonder if he ever did a little dance?

After the fields were the crossings. First the long narrow footbridge that spans the Onny, then the A49 and lastly the railway before trotting up Long Lane westerly towards Wales. Any route west of the Mill has to negotiate river, road, and railway, with various bridges and fords.

Our treks bypassed Craven Arms, once a hamlet known as Newton.

Charlie, Steph, Rach and Nicola riding Jack, Mandela, Avalon, Harvey with Holly the retriever ready to leave Affcot Mill in 1998. The Land Rover Defender on the right was about to embark on its final seaside voyage. Avalon the tall grey mare was due to compete in a 100 - mile endurance event but was vetted out before the start. The issue was of no consequence and her owner sent her on the trek instead

It grew in the early nineteenth century when the railway arrived and was renamed Craven Arms, after the well-established coaching inn dating from Georgian days. The town is now the site of the Blue Remembered Hills Discovery Centre. It is described as "The Gateway to The Marches" and here the railway junction to the Heart of Wales line leaves the Welsh Marches line, on its spectacular passage through mid-Wales.

Another route we historically used passes the beautiful Stokesay Castle after negotiating the A49 crossing.

Stokesay is one of the finest examples of a fortified manor house in Great Britain. It was built c. 1270 – 1280 making it also one of the oldest. It was held for the King in the Civil War, but fortunately surrendered without resistance in 1645 and the order to dismantle it in 1647 was never carried out. It was in a ruinous state for a long time until it was restored in the early twentieth century. There is also a magnificent half-timbered gatehouse. Next to the castle is a church dating in part from Norman times. The Castle, church and lake beside them are popular subjects for photographers.

With the rush of the A49 road being dicey enough, we then encountered the railway at a stop, look and listen crossing. Quite a tricky business with a big group of horses and children. I remember the adults stressing the great importance of having BOTH gates secured open before anybody (other than the gate person, on foot) set foot or hoof on the railway line. We needed an escape route. No rider would ever want to be trapped on the wrong side of a crossing gate if a train thundered through. Even a "bomb-proof" pony would be frightened to the core. When we were all safely through, we would climb steeply up through the woods and head to Aldon

A lot of four-year-old horses, newly backed, trekked to the coast over the years. It was considered the "making of them". After the first 10 miles there was generally a little less of the bolting, spooking and bucking that is often prevalent in a young horse. With lots to see, hear and smell the horses always returned home less green.

Along the way we encountered tractors, pigs, rivers, bridges, railways, dogs, pheasants, cows, crow-scarers, screaming way-farers, soldiers and a colony of wild boar. It was a learning curve, yet the young horses always had the comfort and the security of the herd which they became a part of. Horses from landlocked counties got to test the sand and sea with their hooves. And they all got accustomed to staying the night in an array of different pastures, and sometimes stables.

Likewise, the inexperienced riders quite often came out the other side cantering bareback with the reins in one hand, and a lot wiser at handling the horses from the ground. Avoiding the teeth or the quick hind-foot strike that was usually intended to put another pony in its place, was often a tougher test than staying in the saddle. Ruth remembers setting off on the very first trek to Llangrannog being afraid to canter, in her words "That didn't last long!". Similarly Charlotte had only ridden a few miles at walking pace before she was introduced to the treks and she was just as quick a learner, both girls kept coming back for more over the years!

Even the experienced riders were caught out sometimes. Maz earned himself a bit of a reputation with his actions. Somebody had fallen off him in the sea and Celia grabbed his reins, only to be bitten by him. He also delivered Alison with a hind-hoof strike to the thigh after somebody walked past with a bowl of horse food. Poor Alison revealed a bruise the size of a dinner plate the following day. Maz was a very easy ride, a real gentleman if you were on board, but you most definitely had to be on guard if you were next to his 16hh withers.

From Aldon, curious little narrow lanes would then lead us to Clunbury Hill, where the horses would get the first feel of wind in their manes and grass under their feet. Alive and fresh on a summer's day, with adventure mapped out before us, it was the essence of trail riding at its best. Padded with fine delicate mountain grasses and topped with the familiar tight little copse of conifers, Clunbury Hill is likely home to the animals such as those in the Farthing Wood books. As we dropped down into the quaint and pretty village of Clunbury, spirits were high and limbs not yet sore.

Upon Clunbury Hill, looking over Clunbury village to Clunton Hill 2019

Looking south westerly along the ridge of Clunbury Hill towards Purslow Wood 2019

The horses would see few busy main roads on the treks as we went to great lengths to avoid the risk of being pinned against a hedgerow so that two lorries could pass each other on the carriageway. Our group of children, dogs and often young, green horses meant our routes were not created to get there in the shortest time possible, but rather to utilise beautiful bridleways and avoid as much motorised traffic as we could.

Where the main artery roads of Wales needed to be crossed, we strived to do so without travelling along their length. If this rule had to be broken, in order to keep the herd safe our driver of the day would provide us with a convoy. Driving in front of us to slow the oncoming traffic down. I'm not sure how the police would have dealt with our traffic control but luckily they never came across it. The somewhat higgledy-piggledy route map shows just how indirect the overall route became. The sea was the destination but of course the journey was just as significant.

But returning to the route we later established for the treks... After crossing the A49 we would begin the climb up Long Lane, self-de-

A typical bridleway in the Marches. Hilary on Munchie, Kylee on Shalako, Judy on Mandela and Nicola on Maz, 1995

scriptive and a lot easier on a horse than on a bike I might add, with its unremitting ascent and false summits.

Next we would ride across Hopesay Hill, an "idle hill of summer", to borrow Housman's perfectly fitting stanza. Designated common land and managed by the National Trust, it was home during the years of our treks to a herd of Welsh mares, foals and their accompanying stallion. He was a friendly little fellow and kept his herd tight beside him as we rode past, happy just to watch us disappear without any confrontation. You will read later about another Welsh stallion with a little more interest in our herd.

Hopesay Hill is an idyllic and happy little hill, comfortable and friendly. Fringed to the west with a string of copper beech trees, from its cropped mound you can gaze westward across to Burrow Hill Fort and to the north your eyes may rest on a conical hill sticking out above its surroundings. The conifer forest that cloaks that hill conceals another Iron Age fort, known as Wart Hill settlement. A cluster of Scots Pine trees sit atop the old mound and rabbits graze the grass short like a lawn, making it an idyllic picnic spot, with a great view eastward across Shropshire.

Shropshire is particularly well endowed with hill forts; with 50 known earthworks, just about every hilltop has one in the south western region.

A ride along the Heart of Wales railway is a great way to see all those hilltop forts and earthworks. Steep bumps and humps are strewn throughout the Marches before the train takes you deeper into Wales and towards the Elenydd. After this the scenery changes to vast plateaus and uplands.

Many of the lowland Iron Age settlements have long since been built upon or ploughed but those up high are often still evident. Some historians believe people lived with their animals in these forts whereas others believe they were used only in times of danger. Burrow Hill Fort is believed to have been a settlement of high status due to the presence of two springs and the discovery of pottery believed to have been traded from other parts of Shropshire.

When the mist clings to the floors of the valleys and dales, Burrow can be seen peeping out through the fog like an island, with its oaks atop looking like hazy sepia cauliflower heads. A cluster of land detached from its surroundings by a sea of fog, it harbours ancient stories of defence and the fight for survival.

Here one can imagine families going in and out of their simple wattle and daub round houses with thatched roofs. Goats, sheep, cows, pigs and geese would share the settlement and provide food alongside the crops that were grown. It would be a hive of activity with the smelting of iron and milling of grains. The sounds and smells of the animals, fires and cooking would fill the air around the fort. The voices of children would bounce across the valleys as they ran in and out of the huts and hid in the ditches.

Now you may be lucky enough to see deer on the grassy banks or red kites high above the oak canopies. Burrow rests like a silent and peaceful island in the mist.

From the Fish, a little hamlet whose houses were apparently built from the remains of a monastery where monks practiced aquaculture,

The quirky post at the Fish, a sign we would pass when we took the lane to Hopesay rather than over the hill.

hence its name (and its quirky signpost adorned with a fish), we followed the lane down to the village of Hopesay.

Hopesay has a 13th-century church. Its wooden tower was said to be used by villagers as a hiding place from Welsh invaders. Sadly, its school closed in 1989 along with the post office and shop. Hopesay appears to reside in a perfect little pocket of peace and tranquillity, like many of the other small villages along our route.

The rolling farmland of the Marches is crossed by the Shropshire Way at this point. This was originally created in 1980 as an extension of the Sandstone Trail to take in South Shropshire. It was then revised ten years later and modified and updated over the years. We joined it and rode on towards Kempton

I vividly recall strings of black rotting crows hung in lines along the barbed wire fence that enclosed us on our track here. The heavy scent of rotting, sun-scorched feathers and hide filled the air. Then there was the crow-scarer, firing every few minutes like a gun. Not a place to linger. Unsure where the contraption was, or how long between shots, I would ride rigid with anxiety, waiting for my horse to spook, setting the adrenaline pumping through both horse and rider as if sharing one heart.

Also full of fear is the pheasant, who cowers, hiding quietly in the long grass until the horse is right upon it, only then deciding to screech and flap to escape. It would have surely gone unnoticed had its crouching body of feathers sat tight. Instead it would panic, resulting in our soft looking golden retrievers chasing it down. If it happened to come upon a fence before it could take flight, then the dogs would catch the poor creature and Judy would hop off, ring its neck and strap it to the saddle. It would be plucked (mostly), gutted and frozen or roasted at the next opportunity.

Next on our route came the forest tracks around Bury Ditches Hill Fort, a scheduled monument and described as one of the finest hill forts in Britain. Quite an impressive fort by all accounts, although we tended to just get lost amongst the conifer plantations where every year the paths seemed to change. I have an aversion to such forests which are like a giant monoculture wheat field. A crop. A harvest offering no interaction with its surrounding native flora and fauna, no intricate ecosystem. Symbiotically devoid.

The tracks, tough on hoof and limb, all look the same. They are functional, not designed for horses but for monstrous forestry machines to carry the harvest ripped from the soil.

Of course, I understand our need for such plantations. They provide wood pulp and paper, and there are certain species of birds who make these forests their home. I just prefer to ride quickly on. Maybe I'm spoilt, having been raised at the foot of Wenlock Edge where ancient woodland dominates, with its broad leaved species and rich diverse forest carpet. There are Bluebells, Anemones and Wild Garlic to name just a handful.

Judy writes about Day 1 on the 1989 trek:

> "Joyce, Joan, Sue and Celia, how _could_ you go wrong on so simple a ride? Some of you wanted a faster pace than myself and my four year old Arab and beginner rider Fiona (who later became fearless) from London. So Emily, dearest daughter, took the brave ones on the fast ride so she would not end up arguing with mum about her "slow pace". But the "girls" did not believe that Em knew the way at a certain point so set off another way. Emily, Emma and Polly arrived first, shortly followed by Fiona and me. Meanwhile some of us relaxed and swam in the river Clun at Hurst Mill, home of Joyce and Roy where some of our ponies were to graze that

night. Rob "having kittens" about poor little Timmy (seven years old and just off the lead rein). He did eighteen miles that first day! Joyce, Timmy and Celia and the others arrived about two hours later, but poor Sue and Joan were even further delayed when Joe's pony went lame (on the first day!) and they had to stay at the Engine and Tender, Aston On Clun, to sort that out. Luckily a replacement was provided by another Sue and they all arrived much later on.

Not to worry. Still all friends and a delicious curry cooked by Joyce. Dave, the hostel warden, ate with us. Dear Dave, every year you make us so welcome, filling water buckets for our horses, a smile on your face! Last minute fence jobs – we love you. Rob and Barry joined us for the meal with some light, sparkling refreshments to ease tired limbs."

The following year in 1990, there was a big gang of us comprising Collyers, Elliots, Evans, a Powell and an Osgathorp. There was a consortium of toddlers, teens and in-betweens. Some stayed at the YHA, some at a caravan at Clunton whilst others stayed in a B&B, all dining together at The Crown in the evening. During the later treks we stayed in the town of Clun in a wonderful holiday cottage owned by one of our rider's parents. It was quite a luxury to have a house to ourselves and the horses grazed nearby in a pasture by the ford.

For many years we rode through Sowdley Woods to Hurst Mill near Clun. The tall conifers gave us an easy wide track with glades to enjoy. Stephanie remembers feeling pure bliss and contentment; Sheer happiness as she cantered Mandela along the path. Such a memory to keep and cherish and to share more than twenty years later. In "The Power of Now," a book by Eckhart Tolle, the reader is urged to discover such moments. These moments tend to happen to me when I'm similarly immersed in a beautiful natural landscape, quite often during "the golden hour" on a summer's evening just before dusk.

We ambled down through the tall pines and firs to Hurst Mill, where the horses grazed in the river pastures. My memories are of balmy summers evenings with a fruity scent of pine needles in the air and long shafts of sunlight piercing through the dark canopy making pools of light on the forest floor.

The old mill at Hurst provided grazing for some of the horses. The river Clun wound through the lush fields and I remember swimming in its waters with the other children.

I remember Trigger, a liver chestnut pony who lived there, frequently had his tail chewed off by the cattle. I was mortified in case they did the same to my Lassie's beautiful thick black tail, which had been carefully detangled and oiled before setting off. I was anxious that I might find her looking like a cart horse with a half tail chewed high above where the cart shafts would sit on her flank!

The Campaign for The Protection of England suggests that Clun may be one of the most tranquil locations in England.

A E Housman, the English classical scholar and poet (1859-1936), writes of youth in the English countryside and is best known for his poems in The Shropshire Lad;

> *Clunton and Clunbury,*
> *Clungunford and Clun,*
> *Are the quietest places*
> *Under the sun.*

> *In Valleys of springs of rivers,*
> *By Onny and Teme and Clun*
> *The country for easy livers,*
> *The quietest under the sun*

Clun Hostel is a converted water mill and stables dating in part back to 1772 and last used commercially in 1920. For many years the dormitories were reached using ladders and the YHA archives tell us tales of how it once was…

"the men's wash house is where originally the mill ponies were stabled. The scrubbed, clean white basins fit very neatly in the old trough!"

"Down at Clun, one chilly April, we had the beamed old mill entirely to ourselves, and took advantage of this privacy to heat large quantities of water and have a

stand-up bath before a roaring fire"

"I was unbooked and had to climb in through a window"

"The warden there was fearsome. The hostel had a wood burning stove called Little Cherub"

With electricity coming to the hostel in 1952, and a phone installed as late as 1982, for many years it would have been an unsophisticated and rustic place to stay. We were lucky to have experienced some of this simple living before it was renovated in 2005. It is still a fantastic place to stay, with the mechanical workings of the mill behind screens, safely on show, and a common room in the cobbled pony stalls. Its stairs are narrow and steep, and the window onto the lawn is still used as a door by the kids.

Our horses used to graze freely in the garden amongst the other travellers, and we used to hang out of the upper granary half door through which the bags of flour would have been passed during the building's working life. But now health and safety law has caught up with Clun Mill and the half door is kept firmly locked. The hostelling ethos remains the same and the building remains much the same to look at from the outside, an extension has been built on the side. and some colour is provided by a Crocosmia border.

Judy and Sue preparing the riders packed lunch at Clun youth hostel in 1989

Ready to set off to Bleddfa from Clun Mill in 1993. Tim on Holly, Emma on Selina, Rosie on Bosun, Ross on Prizey, Ruth on foot, Rachael on Misty, Alison on Star and Cherry on Dilly

Clun Mill YHA in 1989 with the granary door swung open above the lawn

Clun is still open as a YHA at the time of writing, whilst many others have sadly closed. The picture right is of Archie and Minnie outside Clun Mill where we stayed for the night during a three day cycling adventure in 2019

Clun YHA. Autumn 2019

Letting the ponies roam on the lawn didn't go without incident. Joyce recalls making tea in the kitchen only to turn around and be face to face with Bronwen, Oliver's (and later Catherine's) Welsh Mountain pony. Bronwen, although looking sweet, had actually earned herself the nickname "Mugger". As soon as you turned your back on Mugger, she would nip you. You always had to be on guard whilst in her company. Her ears would lie flat back and her neck would snake out; the whites of her eyes would show as she bit you wherever she could. She was a dream to ride, never a problem apart from perhaps the odd buck in an open field.

So armed with a frying pan, which was the nearest "shield" to hand, Joyce proceeded to wave the pan at Mugger and try to chase her out. Only Bronwen wasn't ready to leave the building yet and Joyce chased her around the big dining table several times with the frying pan held high. We can't recall if the table was occupied by other hostellers at the time, but Mugger eventually shot out of the front door back to her friends and Joyce enjoyed her cup of tea.

Tim shares some of his memories of the trek in 1993 in the form of a scrapbook written when he was aged 11. He writes about Clun hostel:

> *"Ross and I did so well with our hostel chores that the warden took us through a secret door so that we could see and touch the cogs and other workings of the mill.*
>
> *I made friends with some Australians, one of them was allergic to horses - he couldn't have chosen a worse time to stay. He decided to sleep in his car rather than risk being poorly. That night I got told off by mum because we were pillow fighting and wrestling late. After 21 miles mum thought I should be ready to sleep. BUT I WASN'T."*

Tim and Joyce had covered more miles than the rest of the trekkers as they had ridden from their home in the Corvedale. I do wonder if the Australian chap had witnessed a pony in the kitchen and was worried one might find its way to his bed at night, so that's why he chose the car.

After we had settled into the hostel after our first day in the saddle, having fed ourselves and the horses, we would often walk out to

Clun Castle.

Clun castle was founded shortly after the Norman conquest to demonstrate the authority of the English monarchy over the region. It and the surrounding settlement prospered in the 13th century. It was owned by the Fitzalan family for 400 years during which it suffered a number of attacks from the Welsh, including being burnt down. It became the Fitzalans' hunting lodge by the mid 14th century when they moved their main residence to Sussex. In the early 15th century, followers of Owain Glyn Dwr devastated the surrounding area and by 1539 the castle was reported as ruinous.

Today the tumble-down castle with its soft moat banks and tussocky hills provides the most perfect playground. We giggled and tumbled around in days gone by and children today do the same. A ruin that is un-ruined.

The battles of Clun Castle are now stowed away in the distant past, and as the sun sets behind it on its rocky mound high above the river, the serenity of the scene consumes you.

Clun Castle 2019

The perfect playground. Soft and bouncy with no plastic in sight. Minnie, Ella and Carol in 2019

Clun town is located within the Shropshire Hills Area of Outstanding Natural Beauty which takes up a quarter of the county. Shropshire is indeed beautiful, my bias aside: Natural England designated it officially so in 1958. It has 310 square miles of beauty designated for conservation due to its significant landscape value. Primarily, this blanket of splendour covers the south west region of the county.

Part of this area is known as the Clun Forest, a large upland stretching between the rivers Teme and Clun, from Ludlow up the Clun Valley. It used to be an expanse of ancient woodland and had a status as a Royal Hunting Forest during Medieval times. Only fragments of the forest survive today. It is now characterised as a mixture of pastureland, moorland and mixed woodland.

The region also has its own breed of upland sheep which are hardy, adaptable and long-lived. Clun Forest sheep are bred for their meat, milk and wool, and with their wide pelvic frames they are said to lamb easily.

The town of Clun is divided in two by a 15th century packhorse bridge, the ancient part of the town to the south and the newer Norman town on the north. Unusually for a town, it has never been served by a railway. Maybe this is a contributor to its serenity.

You can see a performance of the Green Man battle with the Frost Queen on the packhorse bridge to bring spring to the Clun valley during its Green Man festival in May. The town becomes a buzzing hive of activity at this time and also in August when a carnival is held.

Stories of riding through the parish of Clun during the 80's and 90's would not be complete without talking again about Bill Lock. I have sourced the following excerpts from an article in the Clun Courier, Number 137, December 2001, written by Doreen Woodford.

We became accustomed to Bill's high pitched shrieks as he walked alongside the ponies and horses many times on plenty of different occasions. Waving his stick and pushing his old pram, he could appear very frightening to the young children; in time he became part of our journeys and really quite familiar.

DEAF AND DIFFERENT BY DOREEN WOODFORD

Bill Lock was born in a Romany Caravan, a member of a very large, extended and well known family. Like some other relatives, Bill was born deaf. From birth he was known as "Dummy" and was sometimes known as "DumDum". In those days, nobody thought anything about using such a nickname and it was not until Bill's later years that a few people started to call him "Bill" (or sometimes "Will"). Whether he noticed the difference, no one will know.

Bill was born in March 1910 in Churchstoke (now Powys, then in Merionethshire). His birth appears not to have been registered, but he was christened William Hubert Lock in the non-conformist chapel (at that time some non-conformist clergy were more willing to baptise Romany babies than the Church of England clergy). Like his two hearing brothers and many hearing sisters, Bill had no schooling and moved around Shropshire, Gloucestershire and Wiltshire and into Wales, with the many familiar caravans of the large family. Like them, Bill accompanied his mother and other women selling pegs and other things from door to door. Bill later learned how to make those pegs

Bill grew to love horses and all his life was good with them. As soon as Bill was old enough, he undertook many kinds of farm jobs with the lads.

Everyone in the family had developed a good wide language of "home signs" as Bill never had the opportunity to learn British Sign Language. These "home signs" were sufficient for people to give him instructions (which he carried out well) and for him to express some of his wants and needs.

The communications Bill had developed did not, ever, give him any meaningful way of expressing either thoughts or feelings. He found some release in a great deal of loud shouting and various "grunts" and "ahs", and Bill could also use facial expressions very well. Those who knew him best and cared most about him mentioned that he communicated with his eyes, showing happiness and unhappiness. His loud shouting sometimes frightened people; some local women and children were very frightened of Bill. This was sad because Bill really loved children; the youngsters in the family would wait eagerly for him to come home and Bill never failed to have sweets in his pockets for them.

At some point in his life, most members of his family eventually moved into houses, but Bill would never sleep inside. He loved his caravan which he kept painted and decorated. Sometimes he slept under it, rather than inside.

The Romany caravans went and Bill lived firstly in a more ordinary caravan and later in various outside buildings in Clun, which belonged to Harry and for a while Kitty. However, Bill always carefully fitted up these buildings so that they were as much like a caravan as possible.

Bill knew where all the family members were and often walked miles to visit them. Bill was known all round a wide area, both because of the family movements when he was young, and also because of his continued walking. Whatever the reactions of the local people, and these ranged from shunning him, despising his background, liking him, fearing him, helping him, caring for him and even loving him, nobody thought he should be somewhere else. Bill Lock belonged to Clun and everyone agreed.

Bill, however, never knowingly hurt anyone, but he had an iron grasp and would hold people by the arm until he had made them understand what it was he wanted.

As he got older, he pushed an old pram on which he brought back many discarded oddments of furniture, old rope, cloth, mattresses and other things.

One set of visitors who probably never came back to visit Clun were the people in a car that stopped on the narrow bridge over the River Clun to ask Bill the way. He put his head in the car and shouted. He frightened them all so much that they drove off with his head still in the car! The walking stick that accompanied Bill everywhere in his middle and old age was wrapped round with colourful tape in his favourite red, blue and yellow colours. Bill always waved his stick with vigour and it became another way of expressing his feelings. Clun has an annual carnival with visits from a well known team of Morris Dancers (The Shropshire Bedlams and Martha Roden's Tuppeny Dish Team). Bill would always join the dance and jig along with them, vigorously waving his stick. He had a good sense of rhythm, jigging to the music of a variety of dance bands that came to the carnival, and lifting his stick pretending to play it like a fiddle (many of Bill's forebears were well-known for their fiddle playing. One was found dead in a very cold winter clutching his fiddle. Some family tombstones have a fiddle on them).

Denys Sharrocks who lived at Mardu wrote a thoughtful and understanding poem about Bill, which of course he could not read. The poem included the lines:

> *"We understand each other in our ways,*
> *Our simple mime sufficed for simple needs,*
> *To quell, that is, your sudden rage,*
> *To ease your anger at the shabby hand*
> *That trickster in the sky dealt out.*
> *No gift of sound of bird or stream or breeze or human voice:*
> *No background music, noises off.*
> *Instead, so many silent movies, captions lost."*

The poem's three verses also refer to Bill's "shrieking cries": to his "bright waistcoat, dandy's trousers" and his "signed O, enough for half a pint" When Bill was 84 years old, the local sculptress (Gemma Pearson) made a sculpture, which gave him great pleasure. Every sitting, as well as the final result, seems to have been an unadulterated pleasure: a great understanding grew between them. This was unusual, as it seems that apart from the family, Bill's friends were all male.

In his late eighties, Bill had a bad fall and was admitted to hospital, where there was a person on the staff who could communicate with him. Bill soon needed more care and had to move into a sheltered bungalow. To everyone's surprise, he accepted this first move "indoors"; eventually he went into a local nursing home where after two months, he died on 18th November 2000.

Bill Lock was buried on 25th November 2000 in the churchyard of St George's Church, Clun, beside the graves of one of his sisters, his aunt and uncle. At least two hundred, if not more, attended the service and burial.

The coffin rested outside the church and the Morris Dance team danced around it.

William Hubert Lock was the last of his kind. There will never be another deaf person like him.

DOREEN E. WOODFORD
Sourced from the Clun Chronicle 2001

The bronze bust of Bill created by Gemma Pearson can be seen at Clun Town Trust Museum.

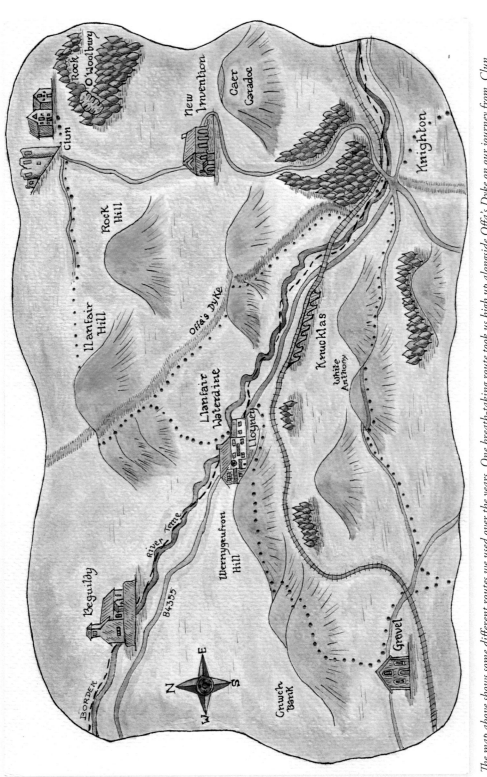

The map above shows some different routes we used over the years. One breath-taking route took us high up alongside Offa's Dyke on our journey from Clun to Knighton. In the earlier treks we left Knighton due south, heading for Cascob and New Radnor. Other times we climbed out of Knighton westward to White Anthony where we raced across the common land. In later years we used the Jack Mytton Way from Clun, dropping down from Offa's Dyke sooner to cross the border at Lloyney. From here we rode up and over the hills to Gravel.

CHAPTER 4

Cymru, Borders Old and New

The Jack Mytton Way was opened in 1993 and travels through nearly 100 miles of Shropshire's beautiful countryside. It is named after John "Mad Jack" Mytton. Living from 1796 to 1834, he was an eccentric Shropshire landowner, MP, horseman, foxhunter, gambler and debauchee. One of the tales about Mad Jack describe him jumping his horse over a dining room table and out through a window onto the lawn. A colourful character beyond doubt, who played practical jokes such as leaving a horse in his tutor's bedroom. With a most definite link to horses it seemed fitting to name the network of bridleways and old roads after this historic Shropshire fellow. Its passage beside Offa's Dyke is just one of its highlights, with others including the Longmynd, Wenlock Edge and the Clee Hills. The Jack Mytton Way joins the dyke just south of the Clun – Clee ridgeway, an antiquity far older than the dyke itself.

Following the dyke for just a couple of miles, the section we rode alongside is considered to be one of the best preserved and impressive sections in the whole length of the dyke. Along this stretch is Llanfair Hill, the highest point the dyke reaches along its entire length, from Prestatyn to Sedbury Cliffs on the Severn.

The 8th Century early Saxon earthwork defence was built under the reign of King Offa and although its purpose is debated, it separated the Anglican Mercia and the Welsh kingdom of Powys. At 150 miles in distance it roughly follows the Welsh/English border today and parts are up to 65 feet wide and 8 feet high.

Offa's Dyke, Clun and Hopton Castles, and the remains of two castles in Knighton contribute to the string of border defences in the region, evidence of its unsettled history.

After Llanfair Hill we would soon branch off to the right, following the Jack Mytton Way which took us down to Lloyney to cross the river Teme where our horses hooves passed over the current border.

Alex having a giggle in the borders, Maz, Hilary and Munchie in the backgound (1995)

On a wet and wild September's day in 2019, I took a walk up onto Offa's Dyke with our spaniel…

Climbing up through the green fields from Burfield farm, I came upon the dyke looming above my shoulder, its earth encrusted with vivid yellow gorse and long thin fingers of broom with their feathered pods thrashed in the wind. Dotted in the soft grasses, delicate purple harebells fluttered, sheltered and thriving under the thorny arms of their neighbours.

As I rose up onto Llanfair (St Mary's Church) Hill, the wind and rain shook me to the core and the dyke became a barren, tussocky mound with no shrubs able to take hold and where any harebell seeds would be blown into oblivion. Stepping down between the dyke and its flanking ditch provided some respite, although on a horse you would still be exposed. A few stunted foxgloves grasped onto the disturbed earth and burrows where the rabbits had been.

A public footpath follows the ridge of the earth mound but appears to be seldom used. Barbed wire fences periodically span the dyke and a large bull watched us from a field, his fence broken, strung along the ground. We moved quickly on into the elements. Wales to the west looking majestic and enticing with its mountainous charm, and England eastward with its hills crowned with forts and its dales splashed with rivers and dotted with villages.

A stile upon the dyke south of Llanfair Hill 2019

Offa's Dyke in the mist near to Llanfair Hill, the dyke's highest point in 2019

A mountain ash by the dyke, small and gnarled yet steadfast, wearing few leaves and only a handful of berries. A crow had used its sparse canopy to rear its young in a nest 2019

We came across an old plough abandoned in what can only be described as a non-arable landscape. At least the ground may plough but the crops would surely be too exposed 2019

Cows graze in the filtered sunlight, a gap between the rain clouds. The dyke is in the foreground daubed with bracken. There is an old homestead marked on the OS map near to this location. It would have been a very exposed homestead with a view eastward into Shropshire.

The Offa's Dyke Path opened in 1971 and follows, or keeps close to, parts of the dyke. This deviation from the actual ditches, together with the barbed wire strung across the footpath on this section, must protect the dyke from erosion caused by too many explorative feet.

I have vague childhood recollections of my mother and her friends' excited voices ringing through the summer air: "It's Offa's Dyke! Here it is!" only to be followed by long afternoons of barbed wire, stiles and timely detours.

The distorted, cactus-like pines and larches, possibly descendants of cones planted in those Anglo-Saxon days, would creak above the long line of horses. Buzzards crying overhead, drawn to the rich picking of rabbits who found the dyke a perfect place to colonise, as we made our way down to civilisation in Knighton.

Joyce, Celia, Joan and Vivien having a picnic on Offa's Dyke 1990

How kind of Offa, King of Mercia, to provide such a comfy mound as a resting place for our tired ladies.

Judy writes about the 1989 trek:

"Tuesday – Again a leisurely day with only eight miles to ride. We break ourselves and our horses into this trek gradually with two short rides on the first two days. Again, two rides, a fast and a slow. Nobody lost today. All picnicked together in a cool glade just before climbing up on to historic Offa's Dyke. Breathtaking two or three miles along the Dyke with views over Knucklas viaduct, the river Teme and Knighton, before descending the hazardous slippery grassy slope to Panpunton Farm where we graze the horses. A lovely meadow with the river Teme winding through and lush grass (even this year). First time all our horses will be turned out together, so we are a bit worried. At Clun we had two separate fields.

A word about our horses – there's Trampus a 14 year old Appaloosa gelding, 15hh with spots and freckles even on his willy. He is a real character, can do circus tricks and guards his mare, Velvet, a 14hh Fell pony, with his life. Troy, a bay 14.2hh hunter type, and 'his' Peggy, a little grey Welsh brood mare for Timmy. She looks as if she has had a few foals but without one at foot this year, she cares for Timmy as though he were her own. These two live together and Troy allows no-one near Peggy. Nutmeg, a 15hh bay seven year old Welsh cob on her own with Joan, pals up sometimes with Troy and Peggy, other times with Trampus and Velvet.

Bosun, Casper and Tinker have all trekked before. Tinker used to live up to his name and be a little imp, bucking people and saddlebags everywhere, rolling when we stopped to open gates, but he must have improved vastly since we hardly notice him anymore. He is Welsh, 6 years old and Ross rides him. Bosun is a half Arab chestnut gelding, 14.3hh, 9 years old and is Sue's pet. He does not like lorries or big vehicles. Casper is a Caspian, a fine little bay, 12.2hh whom Lucy or Ruth ride. Then there is Star, kindly loaned by our DC, strawberry roan, a Welsh pony mare for Rosie or Kenchi. Blue, Joe's borrowed horse, is a nice 15.2hh hunter type who's done eventing – I wonder what he thinks of trekking?

Daffodil, Emma's loaned cob, is huge and not very fit; luckily, we do not go at a great pace. Sadly, she went lame by Glascwm and had to be returned home. Surprisingly, Emma enjoyed riding her, even though she is used to a much finer and lively type. She says she is very comfortable. Then there is my herd, Janie, my beautiful temperamental, marish palomino 15hh, 8 year old Anglo Arab, bred at Affcot (I had her mother and grandmother), ridden by Polly, my niece. My 4 year old chestnut Arab Shalawi, 15.2hh. Emily's ¼ American Saddlebred, ¾ Arab, 16hh leggy 7-year-old proud chestnut gelding, Maz for short. And Sonny, a 4-year-old dark bay cob with a head like a Shire, just broken in and kindly lent to us by Caroline for the trek. He is for Fiona to ride. To start with he is too naughty for her, so Polly, Emily and Rosie have to sort him out.

Oh yes, we also took Sadie, Em's golden retriever, who even found the time to chase rabbits as well as run with us.

They all keep to their groups in the large field at Knighton and there are no kicks or bites. Knighton Youth Hostel, the old school in the centre of the town is formal after Clun, but very clean and modern. Sue was driving that day and prepared a lovely meal of different cold meats, salads and spuds – yum! Just right for this hot weather. Come on kids, time to wash up. Card playing, Joan and I pouring over the maps for tomorrow's route, teenagers sounding out the local talent, but all tucked up by 11 o'clock"

The Welsh Border. Depictions of skirmishes and unrest throughout history spring to mind. A long string of political and national disputes. Now hardly noticed as people freely cross over the thresholds each way. Our horses stepped across the imaginary line first at Knighton, then in later years at Lloyney.

Interestingly, the river Teme has naturally altered its course since the Laws in Wales Acts and so the border in the Teme valley no longer follows the centre of the river as it once did but stays on what was the course of the river when the border was fixed by the Acts of 1535-1542.

On the other side of the river Teme, is the village of Llanfair Waterdine which sits on the southern edge of the Clun forest. It was historically in Wales, lying to the west of the dyke.

Often the driver would ring the Lloyney Inn and order us all chips, which we gratefully ate as we relaxed with the horses on the green outside the pub.

Rach, Charlie, Judy and Nicola at Lloyney in 1998

Rested and refreshed at the border at Lloyney, about to climb up into the Radnor Forest hills on route to Bleddfa. Rach, Charlie, Nicola and Steph upon their rather laid-back looking horses Avalon, Harvey, Mandela and Jack. Once on the open hillside, spirits would soon change (1998)

More refreshments at Lloyney in 1999. This time Hercules is taking refreshments from Beth's water bottle. Kate and Lewis are with them.

The river Teme whose source is in the Kerry Hills weaves in and out of Wales and England until it eventually becomes an English river as it flows from Knighton on to Ludlow before joining the Severn at Worcester.

Like the Teme, Knighton also has a dual English/Welsh nature, with a small part of the town including the railway station being a part of Shropshire.

Knighton, or Tref-y-clawdd is translated as "The town by the Dyke" and is a small market town nestled under Panpunton and Kinsley Wood. It has the remains of two Norman castles built in the 12th century which were destroyed in 1402 by Owain Glyndwr along with much of the town. It was a centre for wool trading in the 15th century and later an important point on two drovers' routes from Montgomery to Hereford and Aberystwyth to London. The railway reached Knighton in 1861 and the station was built in 1865. It was only made viable due to local landowners and businessmen forming The Knighton Railway Company.

Knighton's striking Victorian Gothic clock tower built in 1872. It stands at the junction of High St, Broad St and West St (2019)

The Horse and Jockey at Knighton. Originally a 14th Century coaching inn. With Kinsley Wood as the back-drop (2019)

Joyce recalls settling the horses to graze in the pastures of Panpuntun after a day's riding in 1990. Vivien's horse, Conker was renowned for his character and was once found dangling his legs over a stable door at a B&B. Knighton saw him up to more mischief. Conker was playing up Vivien, who was undoubtedly tired after a long day in the saddle. "I'll take care of this," rang Sam's voice across the valley. Shortly afterwards Conker dragged Sam swiftly into the river Teme.

The last quarter of a mile along the dyke to Panpuntun Farm, where for many years we grazed the horses is incredibly steep and we often led our horses down to give their backs a rest at the end of the day.

Catherine, Matthew and Sue on their way down from Offa's Dyke (Photo by David Elliott 1990)

Cooling down in the river Teme at Panpuntun, Knighton (Photo by David Elliott 1990)

Bringing in the Arabs for their morning feed in 1990. Myself riding Shally with Camille and Maz following (Photo courtesy of Jane Osgathorp)

1990 was a hot year and we were a big group of riders. Sue on Lizzy, Edward on Tenpee, Catherine on Carrots, Louise on Bossy Boots, Abi on Tango, Barry on Charlotte, Judy on Shally, Myself on Maz and Rosie on Camille. Ready to leave Panpuntun farm (Photo courtesy of Jane Osgathorp)

The essential supervision at feed times. Catherine, Abigail and Jane in the forefront resting with their ponies after a long day's riding. (Photo courtesy of David Elliott 1990)

The rich colours of the chestnuts and a bay on a scorching day in 1990. Abi on Tango, Louise on Bossy Boots, Rosie on Shally and Emily on Maz. These were the only 4 horses to complete the whole distance that year (Photo courtesy of Jane Osgathorp)

The hostel building used to be a village primary school and opened as a YHA hostel in 1979. Situated halfway along the Offa's Dyke Path, it received funding from the Countryside Commission. It was closed in 1992 due to a large crack in a structural wall and has since been privately owned.

Next door to the old hostel building today is Offa's Dyke Visitor Centre, which opened in 1999. When I walked around the hostel building 20 years later in 2019, there was a collection of weird and wonderful steel sculptures on display. It had become the workshop of Andy Hazell, a Public Artist – Automatist – Photographer and Film – Maker. He has a fascinating website and pictured below are a few of his creations I happened to see over the wall.

The routes taken from Knighton to Glascwm varied over the years. At one point we would climb up steeply from the town on a little lane that led to White Anthony Common with spectacular views and Knucklas viaduct again on show, spanning the valley. Then the lane dropped down to Llangunllo, where we started the crossing of Radnor Forest. Other times we headed due south out of Knighton roughly following the course of Offa's Dyke, until we headed south westerly to Cascob then New Radnor, through Radnor Forest on its eastern flank. Sometimes on the return trip we rode straight home from Knighton rather than staying at Clun. This route would take us via Bucknell, Darky Dale and Shelderton

After 1992, when Knighton hostel had closed and we started to take accommodation at Treboeth, Bleddfa, our route changed so that we navigated Radnor Forest on its western side. From the border at Lloyney we climbed up Goytre Hill, then onto Wernygeufron with the railway winding along the valley below us to the south and Beacon Hill rising high to the north. We had a good couple of miles of cantering along wonderful bridleways before descending into Gravel where we rode under the railway and entered into Radnor Forest.

Climbing up Goytre Hill after crossing the Welsh border at Lloyney. 'Goytre' in Welsh is 'Coed-tre' and can be translated as 'house in the wood'. Steph, Rach and Charlie riding Jack, Avalon and Harvey in 1998

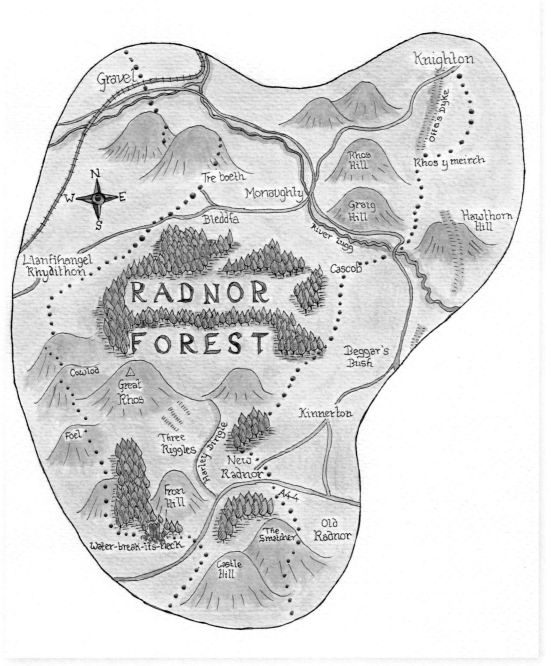

The map above shows two of the routes we took through Radnor Forest. Great Rhos, which we contoured on a beautiful bridleway, is the highest point above sea level on the route we took across Wales

CHAPTER 5

Radnor Forest

Much like Clun Forest, Radnor Forest is a forest only in the medieval sense, of an unenclosed hunting ground. The parts we rode through were open hillside with beautiful views in all directions. It is a group of mountains consisting of a central *massif* almost cut in two by Harley Dingle.

With the Heart of Wales railway and the river Lug marking the northern edge of Radnor Forest, the village of New Radnor marks its southern edge. It is said to be the least populated area in the UK apart from the Outer Hebrides.

Soon after entering the forest, in the years after Knighton YHA closed, we dropped down from the hillside straight into the yard at Treboeth, our accommodation.

Treboeth can be translated as "warm house", the name could not suit the place any better. It was a warm, buzzing hive of hospitality and farm life. Margaret and Bob Gardiner bred wild boar and owned a pack of Irish Wolfhounds. They were also horse lovers and enjoyed to hunt. The food Margaret prepared was always fantastic, especially when washed down with plenty of fine wines. To us, it was a bit of a treat not to be squeezed in a dorm with fellow hostellers. A delicious heart-warming breakfast was always given to us in the morning, to prepare us for our ride over the hills to Glascwm.

Rachel B still makes the famous "Bleddfa Cake". Introduced to us and made by Margaret, it is an almond sponge cake with an almond and treacle topping.

We also had the rare option of stabling some of the horses at Treboeth if we liked and although they mostly grazed on the hill, it was great to have a yard, tack room and ample space for our preparations.

In 2000, whilst riding from Clun, my town-reared retriever Kizzy surprised us by catching a pheasant. This was shortly followed by Holly catching a partridge. After a couple of quick tweaks to finish the birds off, Judy tied them both to her saddle and we rode into Treboeth yard. I'm not certain whether they were plucked that evening but Margaret agreed to Judy keeping them in her freezer until the next morning. I'm also uncertain who found the birds in the freezer at a later date when it became clear Judy had accidentally picked up two bags of frozen mince instead. Maybe Margaret had to change her menu from Chilli to Game Pie one night.

Judy has always been a hunter-gatherer. Once she filled her jumper with puffballs, shaking them up all day long as she trotted and cantered along, but in the end the riders were all too scared to eat them in case they were poisonous.

Charlie and Margaret with Mav and Finagan, the wolf hounds 1998

Karen gets a warm welcome by Salome and the pack at the "warm house" 2000

Alison fusses one of the huge dogs in 1991

Charlie and Tracey with Mave, Esker and Finagan 2000

*Kate and Beth
with the hounds
in 1999*

Bleddfa in 1991. From the left, Ruth riding Casper bareback, Judy on Maz, Alison G (was Moore) holding Shally with his bandaged knee, Alison on Jack, and Rosie on Kasha. Holly with a new friend in the forefront.

The 1991 trek didn't start too well at all. Casper's girth had been rubbing giving him a sore, which meant Ruth either rode him bareback or he was led from another horse. Ruth was riding Shally when he tripped and skidded on his knee. Ruth also skidded on her knee causing friction burns from her nylon jodhpurs. Shally cut his knee badly and luckily Alison managed to bandage it, being first aid trained for her teaching profession. The brand new western saddle that I bought back from the USA also got scratched during poor Shally's fall. These incidents happened in the first couple of days. The photographs of this small group of trekkers along the way, however, always show them smiling. They appear to be such a content little group.

Throughout the 18 years of sea bound treks, and with all the different people involved, there were inevitable frictions between personalities; a degree of tension was bound to rear its head, especially when people were tired and hungry. I've not been told of any major quarrels though, other than my mother hitting me with a broom at Knighton during my testing teenage years. There was the snoring which deprived many people of much needed sleep; I believe that rattled a few nerves as well as bed posts, but I couldn't possibly say who was responsible.

We always left Treboeth, Bleddfa feeling alive and refreshed, maybe sometimes a little hungover too, but what better cure than the air of the Radnor Forest on horseback. First though we had to negotiate a section of winding, busy, main road. It was the only really dicey section where if lorries came they would have little time to react to the horses and there were no verges for us to escape onto. The section was only a couple of hundred feet long and joined two beautiful bridleways. I always remember feeling incredibly anxious, as often our horses were young and green. Judith's solution was to have the Land Rover driven ahead of us, straddling the central double white lines with its hazard lights flashing. It worked perfectly well for slowing down the oncoming wagons and luckily the lorries that came up behind us were slowed down by the incline of the road.

So it really did feel like a great relief when we left the tarmac and crossed the majestic mountains.

A vast and beautiful area consisting of valleys, mountains and forests, is a horse rider's dream. Its highest point is Great Rhos with its peak at 2166 feet, and whose western upper flank we rode across, marking our highest point of elevation on our complete 126 mile trek to the coast. Black Mixen, Whimble, and the Three Riggles, are rather less Welsh sounding peaks and features, and Harley Dingle is a valley used for testing weapons. There is a danger zone in Radnor Forest relating to this valley, which lies the other side of the Great Rhos to our route down the western side.

With Great Rhos above our left shoulders, the noses of Cowlod, Foel and Rhiwiau stretched to the east in a line before their sides dropped steeply down to the valley where Penybont sits and the river Ithon meanders. Another three miles of beautiful hillside to canter across, stopping to take in the spectacular viewpoint near Foel where plenty of photos were taken over the years. We then rode through Warren Wood, which hides the aptly named "Water break its neck" a 68 feet high waterfall, slightly to the north of our trail. Then we crossed the A44 west of New Radnor leaving the spectacular Radnor Forest until we were to return 5 weeks later. The views are extraordinarily different when travelling in the opposite direction.

Legend tells us that the local people built four churches around Radnor Forest to contain the last dragon in Wales, who lay sleeping in the area. The churches in Cefnllys, Dolau, Nant Melan and Cascob were all dedicated to St Micheal (Welsh ; Mihangel), who was the victor over the dragon. Some people believed that the dragon would awaken if any of those churches were destroyed.

Tracey on Mooney and Karen on Beau. On a drovers' road in Radnor Forest in 2000

Judy and Hilary riding Mandela and Munchie in Radnor Forest in 1995. Over their right shoulders is Fron las Dingle, with the land behind stretching westwards to the coast. To their east behind the photographer is Great Rhos. The track they are on is approximately 1788 ft above sea level and the highest point on our trek route. The riders would sometimes get a glimpse of the sea some three days or so before the end of the journey, then would not see it again until the final day. On a clear day the first sighting may have been from here in the Radnor Forest

Ruth and Rosie riding Maz and Mandela in the same location in 1994

Same place, Tim riding Holly in 1993

Tracey and Charlie with Jack, Mandela and Zac in 1999

Trek 2000, Tracey, Jenny and Karen with Mooney, Mandela, Zac and Beau, Radnor Forest

Map showing the route over the Glascwm Hills down to the Erwood crossing. Gwaunceste Hill is the second highest peak of the whole route westward to the Irish Sea.

CHAPTER 6

Glascwm Hills

When we crossed the A44 after the waterfall, we left the stunning Radnor Forest and traversed the equally breathtaking collection of hills - sometimes referred to as the Painscastle Hills - that took us to Glascwm, where we would stay the night. The hills are a southern offshoot of the Radnor Forest range and the highest point on them is the summit of Gwaunceste Hill.

We passed medieval pillow mounds where artificial warrens were once built to house rabbits for their fur and meat, of which there are numerous across the Welsh landscape. Then we rode past the ruins of Black Yatt farmhouse. With its south gable end still standing in 2007, it was deserted in the mid 20th century and blown up in the 1960s when it featured in a film about the second world war.

Whilst riding across the splendid Gwaunceste Hill (1778 ft) which lies to the north of the range, I would have been unaware that on 25th April 1942 a German Junker 88 plane was shot down by a fighter from Shropshire. Two of its pilots were killed and the remains were brought down from the hill to a barn in Llanhalo Farm. A military funeral took place a few days later. A simple wooden cross can be found tucked in behind a bell at the west end of the nave in the local church in remembrance. The pilots were subsequently interred at a German war cemetery at Cannock Chase.

How dark and terrifying the atmosphere must have been during such times. Such a stark contrast to the heady pleasure we felt as we cantered across its green hills in the summer sunshine.

Here follows Judy's account of our journey from Knighton YHA to Glascwm YHA one Wednesday in the Summer of '89:

> *"Off again in the morning after jobs done at the hostel, walk to the farm, feed, groom, tack up. James, tack up Velvet will*

you, I'm not your groom!' Celia's voice rings out in the cool, sunny morning.

A longer ride today, 22 miles. Timmy and Peggy are going on wheels. My turn to drive – shop for spaghetti bol in Tuffins, with Kenchi and Tim. Emily, Sue, Lucy and Ruth, you've all done this ride before, Emily at least four times, so you <u>must</u> know the way, plus Joan is a fab map reader. All ok 'till the last four miles when you missed the drovers road off the mountain and came off on to the lane too soon. Never mind, it is a very pretty lane.

Naughty, nameless girls (not just teenagers, a mum amongst them) who galloped on ahead leaving God knows what turmoil behind. Also leaving a chalked message on the road: 'Slow as a snail, fast as a hare, maybe one day we'll see you there!' Good thing I wasn't there, or I would have had a tantrum. Down the steep hill to the hostel for spaghetti bol, in the depths of the Welsh mountains. The hostel, an old village school. Relaxed atmosphere, dear Mrs Davies trotting up with boxes of matches for us. Ponies happy (hope stallion not around this year. That is another story for another time).

Come on kids, wash up. Go over route for tomorrow with Joan – 40 miles! We will keep together, no bombing off. Hope I don't get lost with them over that first bit of mountain above Rhulen, where tracks disappear. Joan is fab with the compass, please keep me on course. Memory doesn't help a great deal when you are on top of the world with sky, bracken and sheep as your landmarks."

Glascwm can be translated as "blue valley" and it is an exceptionally quiet little village. When we dropped down from those magnificent hills it felt like riding into another world. A secret world bathed in tranquillity. Akin to Middle Earth perhaps, especially when I spotted a little bent-over old lady carrying a basket of sticks, hurriedly going about her business, fearfully glancing at us, with our herd of horses then quickly rushing away. Oliver teased me, telling me she was a witch when I was young and I was haunted by this story for years.

Its peaceful air must have been the antithesis to the vibe in the village when the droves came through. The Welsh had been driving their livestock across Wales to England since medieval times and up until the 18th century there would have been the threat of wolves. By the end of the 18th century droving was well established.

The Drovers' Roads of Wales written by Fay Godwin and Shirley Toulson is a wealth of information about drovers and their routes. On the back cover they paint a wonderful picture of bygone years:

"Through the heart of Wales run innumerable centuries-old tracks - many still traceable and open. They are the Drovers' Roads. For hundreds of years - from the Middle Ages to the victory of the railways around 1900 - they were trodden by tens of thousands of cattle, sheep and even geese being driven - at an average of 2 mph - to the markets of London. The drovers - many of them now Welsh folk legends -avoiding the main roads, walked their flocks through villages, lively market towns, sometimes following Roman and even earlier highways, passing ancient sites and megaliths and through some of the most dramatic landscapes of Wales."

Drovers passed through Glascwm up until 1913, and the last droves were believed to be the mountain ewes on their journey from Tregaron to Harrow on The Hill. At one point there were as many as four drovers' inns providing lodgings and pastureland for the cattle, men, horses and dogs that would typically make up a drove. The village lay on the route from Builth Wells to Newchurch after which they would likely have travelled on to Hereford and its markets. Often cattle, sheep, turkeys and geese were driven as far as London and even Kent.

It wasn't until the implementation of the railway system during the 1860's that droving declined. Routes changed in line with the railheads so that journeys could be finished by rail.

In 1864 the Mid Wales Railway was built from Newtown to Brecon, via Erwood. The Central Wales Line, which we now know as the Heart of Wales line, was laid from Craven Arms, reaching Knighton in 1861, Builth 1866 and Llandovery in 1868. The Mid Wales railway closed in 1960 but the latter remains open and is mostly single track.

The Heart of Wales line was a constant companion on the first part of our trek route, until we turned northerly near Cynghordy. The railway with its eight or so trains a day would pop in and out between the hills and valleys, showing us its viaducts, the trains sounding their whistles.

There is now a Heart of Wales walking trail that weaves 141 miles along the length of the railway. Completed in 2019, it can be done in sections to suit the walker, using the train to get back to accommodation after the day's exploration.

Many of the drovers' routes were "upgraded" with tarmac and are now our West to East country lanes, A and B roads or even dual carriageways. Many more have been lost to plantations, reservoirs, used for military purposes or lost and forgotten, but others are still there to explore and follow as public rights of way. The trek route joins sections of some beautiful old historic drovers' tracks, and if you close your eyes and ponder whilst on such a section, you can almost hear and smell the cattle.

Droving was not a quiet peaceful affair by all accounts. Smaller droves would all converge on a central meeting place to make a large drove of up to three hundred beasts. There was much shouting, so everyone would have heard them coming. "Heiptro Ho!" they would call in order to warn the local farmers who would need to secure their own stock. Children from the rural homesteads would run to the tops of hills in excitement to watch.

The cattle would have predominantly been the Pembrokeshire breed, who lived on fresh air on the Welsh plateaus. They were coal black with a clean light head and a prominent eye, and sure-footed and agile enough to travel the long distances required over tricky terrain.

Welsh writer and broadcaster Phil Carradice in his blog about Drovers of Wales says:

"In 1794 over 10,000 cattle were exported from Ynys Mon – by 1810 that figure had risen to over 14,000 – and there are wonderful descriptions of the cows swimming in one dark mass across the Menai Straits. Castlemartin Blacks, the almost mythical South Pembrokeshire cows, were particularly sought after and it is on record that, in 1804, at one fair or market in Cilgerran over 20,000 cattle were seen, waiting to be driven away to England."

The lead drover would have likely been accompanied by other men and boys, some on foot and others riding. The ponies would be sturdy Welsh mountain ponies which were descendants of the Arab pack horses brought over by the Romans, or Welsh Cobs.

There would have been dogs accompanying the drovers too; apparently corgis were used as they could nip at the heels of the cows when needed yet be too low to the ground to be struck by a hoof. The dogs were often sent back home when the destination had been reached and they reportedly found their way back, often staying at the same lodgings on their return trip. The droves typically moved at about 2 mph, which included grazing times, and travel was forbidden on a Sunday. The west coast of Wales to Warwickshire might have taken about 16 days.

The routes became a bit like silk roads bringing goods and tidings from the rest of the UK. We're told it was the drovers who brought the news of the British victory at Waterloo and who introduced new and wondrous things such as redcurrants from Kent to Wales.

The many drovers' inns and lodgings found across Wales signs of their history. Often next to remnants of inns are areas of bright green pasture amidst barren land, which is where large quantities of beast fertilised the soil for generations. The term "halfpenny field" refers to the price a drover would pay per head of cattle per night in such a field. Similarly, Smithfield (of which there must be a street or square named after in nearly every sizeable town in Wales) is the English term for cattle market.

The landowners who wanted to advertise their accommodations used to plant Scots pine trees as way markers. Many of whose descendant trees are still there to be seen today, risen from fallen cones, growing as tall as their ancestors and witnessing years of travel and change, harbouring stories that historians try to stitch together.

Then there are the green lanes, often 14ft wide, either hedged, walled or merely sunken with the passing of thousands of hooves. They are a perfect find for those exploring the old routes.

The cattle would often need to be shod especially when they reached the metalled roads of England. There would be various shoeing stations along the routes and the drovers would also carry spares. The half-moon metal shoes to fit the cloven hooves were called "cues".

It is claimed that the geese and turkeys sometimes wore leather boots or had tar stuck to their feet to enable them to make the distance.

Watering spots were crucial, therefore influencing the routes. And dog legs in the often very wide tracks, would provide shelter for the cattle during foul weather.

The drovers would also have to be on the lookout for thieves when they returned from England carrying the money they'd exchanged for their livestock. Llandovery is home to a pub called the Kings Arms, part of which is an old drovers' lodging: On this site the Black Ox Bank was founded in 1799 by David Jones, who started business at age just 15. The notes were embellished on the left hand side with a Welsh black ox, and the bank provided much needed safe keeping of the money bought back from England. The Bank of Llandovery, as it was nationally known, was passed down through the generations until finally in 1909, it was bought by Lloyds Bank marking the end of independent banking in Wales, and the ox was replaced with the black horse emblem that we see today.

Therefore, the quiet little village of Glascwm is steeped in the history of Wales as part of the age old tradition of droving. Today there are no pubs or shops. Alongside its settlement of houses there sits St Davids Church and a village hall. It was said to have been founded by the saint himself in the 6th century and hosts a "magic portable bell" which belonged to St David and was called Bangu. Legend tells us that a woman secretly sent the bell to her husband to secure his release from prison in Rhayader castle, but his captors seized the bell and refused to set him free. On the same night the whole town except the wall the bell was hung upon was consumed by fire.

The Old School building in Glascwm was opened in June 1901 with 15 children and remained open until 1945. It re-opened as the youth hostel in 1947 and remained so for the next 50 years. During 10 of those years we were privileged to stay in the hostel until its closure in 1997.

For me, the youth hostel evokes many memories of extremely garlicky spaghetti Bolognese cooked by Judy. It became an annual feast and possibly helped with the midge situation the following day.

I remember in that tall lofty school hall, then the hostel kitchen, feeling a searing pain in my neck and flicking a wasp or a bee away.

When I found a mirror, I was horrified to find its sting still in embedded in my skin and I'm sure it was still pumping.

Meanwhile outside in the summer's evening, Rachael and Rosie remember all the kids daring each other to climb into the tunnel that carried the stream underneath the village. They would crawl along its dark eerie course entering near the field and out again at the hostel. Our adventures needed no playground with swings and climbing frames.

It was also here that my cousin Polly and I first discovered our ponies had become butter churners when the flasks of milk in our saddle bags had partially turned into butter. Beautiful lumps of creamy butter, a result of cantering across the hills of Wales.

Glascwm indeed holds many memories. Alison and Steve adopted some stray cats who used to hang around the hostel begging for food. By all accounts Judy shut them in the phone box one evening whilst we had our dinner. Feeling sorry for the cats (whose future was in question as the hostel was due to close for the season and there would be nobody to care for them after we left), Alison and Steve hatched a plan. They happened to be driving the next day, so as soon as the riders set off they promptly and swiftly drove the cats to their home in Telford before meeting the riders for lunch. They never told any of the trekkers until years later, and the cats had a wonderful life in suburbia, living to a ripe old age.

Rosie, Ruth, Jane, Judith and Julia ready to set off from Glascwm in 1991 (Photo courtesy of Jane Osgathorp)

Outside Glascwm youth hostel, ready to leave for Llanwrtyd Wells in 1995. Hilary on Munchie, Judy on Mandela, Alex on Maz (Alex bought Maz from us and lovingly looked after him for the rest of his life) and Kylee riding Shalako.

Judy and Jane preparing the packed lunches at Glascwm in 1991 (Photo courtesy of Jane Osgarthorp)

Of all the incidents that happened in that quiet, remote little village, the blue valley nestled in the hills, there is one that had a marvellous ending…

After a night in the dormitory, it was time to walk down the village and up the little path to catch the horses for their morning feed. There in the field mounted on top of Lassie, was a wild Welsh stallion! There was much panic and shouting "There's a strange horse in the field! Mum! Look! What's it doing?!" Confusion as everybody tried to work out what to do, although, what really could anyone do? Rosie vividly remembers being wide eyed with shock and Judy heartily laughing and shouting, "What better sex education could you ask for!" So, we waited for the plucky little section A stallion to finish the job and my little mare gave birth to Summer Surprise 11 months later - a beautiful little blue roan filly conceived in the blue valley. We called her Prizey for short, and she went on to take part in treks herself when she was old enough to be ridden. She turned out to be a pretty, kind little mare and my Lassie made a wonderful doting mother.

Rosie with Summer Surprise (Prizey) as a yearling

When Glascwm youth hostel finally closed its doors to travellers in 1997, we found accommodation in local B&B's, sometimes in Glascwm and other times over the hills in Rhulen.

The next day of riding was a long day in the saddle. It was 31 miles to Bryn Poeth Uchaf youth hostel where we took a rest day. In later years we stayed in a hotel in the centre of Llanwrtyd Wells reducing the distance to 27 miles, provided we didn't take a wrong turn. The first section of the day involved similar terrain to the previous day, straight from the hostel up onto Glascwm Hill. Open, grassy and always sunny as I remember it! Familiar names of landmarks like Mawn and Doctor's Pools were marked off as we cantered through the beautiful open countryside.

We would then briefly join an old drovers' road at Pentre on our way to the village of Rhulen, the route would have taken the droves easterly to Newchurch. An ancient tree canopied holloway at Pentre is testament to the passing of hundreds of hooves.

Rhulen is a tiny village in a steep valley with a tiny church dedicated to St David that has an odd coffin shaped door. The population has decreased over the last few hundred years from 140 in 1820 to around 30 in 2017. It is a quiet hamlet nestled deep in the Radnorshire hills.

From Rhulen we rode up and around Rhulen Hill past the "dancing ground", so called because it is there that the fairies dance! Then we traversed Llandeilo Hill to Cradle Rocks, some say they were called this because the nearby giants had thrown the rocks out of their babies cradles. The next landmark was Twm Tobacco's Grave situated at a boundary stone where two paths cross. There is some mystery to who Twm Tobacco was and why he would be buried at this spot. One story has him as a well-loved packman buried either where he fell, or at his favourite spot. He may have travelled with a pony or donkey selling silk scarves, trinkets and tobacco. Another tale has him as a felon, hanged at the crossroads and then buried in un-consecrated ground.

Before we left the hills and dropped down to cross the river Wye at Erwood, we passed close by to Aberedw Rocks. At the base of the rocks is Llewellyn's cave. Prince llewellyn ap Gruffydd was known as the last prince of an independent Wales before its conquest by Edward I of England. It's said that during the remaining days of his struggle he took shelter from the English in this cave.

He was subsequently killed near Builth Wells in 1282. The cave is surrounded by ancient woodlands and is full of carvings stretching back centuries.

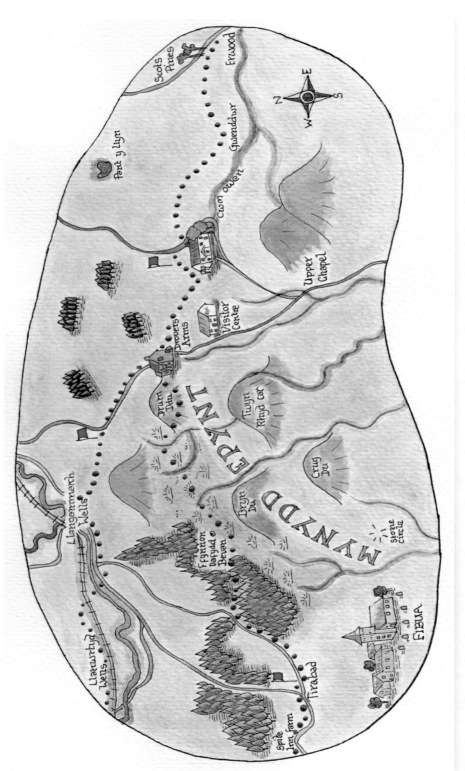

Map showing the initial southernmost route taken across the range where we succumbed to treacherous bogs before finding solid ground at Tirabad, and the northern route which became the safest crossing where we abandoned our pursuit of bridleways and used the military roads.

Chapter 7

Erwood Crossing and The Epynt

Erwood or Er'ood is a corruption of Y Rhyd which means 'the ford'. Erwood crossing marked the lowest point in our route (apart from our final descent to the beach) at just 370 ft above sea level.

This point on the river Wye was also a popular crossing point for drovers. It has a tragic story in its history that dates back to before 1861 prior to when the first bridge crossing was built. A local man named Twm and his son, owned the Boat Inn on the river bank and they also ran a ferry across the wide waters. The basic boat was believed to be a wooden box that was hoisted backwards and forwards with a loop of rope. It would carry up to four cattle when the water was too deep for the drovers to cross. Legend has it that during a crossing when the river was full and swirling, one of the beasts panicked and overturned the boat. The drovers grabbed on to the tails of their animals and were saved but Twm drowned.

Erwood was once a part of the Mid Wales Railway. The station was opened in 1864 and became amalgamated with the Cambrian railway in 1901. Due to a weight limit elsewhere on the line it was traversed by engines of 14 tons or less. On 30th December in 1962 during one of Wales's worst winters on record, the last train was run in heavy snow before the line was closed for good, the following day.

Today Erwood station is a privately run contemporary applied arts gallery. The tea room and exhibitions are inside three railways carriages from the 1880's. Outside on the old platform are restored carriages and a raised cattle dock can be seen together with historic cranes and machinery. A signal box from Newbridge On Wye station was found on a farm being used as a chicken shed. The box was restored and put at Erwood - on loan from its owner and is now used as a bird and bat observatory.

To the left can be seen the raised cattle dock at Erwood station 2019

The restored signal box at Erwood station now used as a bat and bird observatory

The river Wye from Erwood bridge, 1989. A glimpse of what the drovers and their ox had to contend with before a bridge had been erected. A ferry was believed to have been used downstream, in the deeper waters, to the south of where the bridge stands today.

A fuller river Wye in the Autumn of 2019 - Erwood was one of the few crossing places along the Wye suitable for the drovers to use, and a boat was available during floods.

Overlooking Erwood positioned amidst ancient earthworks on Twyn y Garth is a German field gun. It was bought by Nessa Williams Vaughan to commemorate the end of the first World War and in memory of her brother and other local men who were killed in the war. Nessa died in a motor accident before the gun was delivered by rail in 1920, however after some rivalry between the boys of Erwood and those of Llandeilo Graban, it was dragged by men and horses to the old camp on the Twyn Y Garth hill where it was cemented in place. By some accounts it was deliberately aimed at the Wheelwrights Arms in Erwood. After some deterioration over the years it was renovated in 2000. The howitzer would have been capable of firing a 40lb shell 4.3 miles.

On the other side of the river, the ridge of the Twmpath (translated as "mound" and not actually a path) rose up and away from the Wye Valley, into the face of the ancient drovers' route.

Imagine the shock of meeting a herd of 300 black oxen, slipping and slithering their way down the gully to the ford. Or geese gaggling madly with their tarred feet. Sunken roads known as ''holloways' would be formed when hundreds of hooves sliced and churned up the earth. The rains would then wash away the loose soil and the bedrock would be revealed.

I sometimes envisage the droves like a herd of wildebeest on their migration, the group mentality, the pushing and shoving. The adrenaline. Then I sigh at the fundamental difference whereby unlike the wildebeest travelling in search of food, the Welsh beasts were being driven to their own fate. Then I consider the essential health and fitness of each cow in order for it to make that journey, and I surmise that their quality of life would be a cut above the poor beasts that are factory farmed in parts of this world today. I can't imagine there was much of a carbon footprint by the drovers or their cattle, at least until they started to travel by steam train, which started to smog up our atmosphere followed by, of course, the combustion engine.

On the other hand, what would the drovers have thought of us on our Thoroughbreds, Arabs and Hunter types alongside the sturdy mountain ponies much like their own? How would they make sense of our trip, a leisure activity? A holiday we were taking for fun and pleasure. Why were we not working, tending our farms and families? Quite the antithetical scenario.

Slightly to the north of the Twmpath rests an 8 acre lake known as Pant y Llyn, translated as lake in a hollow. An upland lake set in remote and stunning surroundings, it offers anglers the chance to catch hard fighting wild carp. It is referred to as a hidden lake, by such anglers, and was apparently stocked by monks hundreds of years ago.

Mary and Judy riding Jack and Mandela on the return trip, this time heading down towards the Erwood crossing in 1998. Note the Scots Pine trees up on the ridge behind them. Scots Pines were planted as way markers for the drovers to advertise accommodation and pasture. The pines in the photos are most likely descendants of originals planted hundreds of years ago for this purpose.

The same Scots Pines 21 years later and much taller on a misty morning in 2019

Alex on Maz and Judy on Mandela looking back down into the Wye Valley with the river flowing far below, 1995

Beth riding Hercules with Cassie following at the same spot in 1999

Up and up the Twmpath we climbed, the river far below us as we followed the lanes to our picnic spot near Fron Farm. It was a grassy bank where the tiny lane zig zagged providing common land in between. There was plenty of space for the horses to graze and the riders to relax. A running stream at the bottom of the dingle provided water for the horses to drink and there was ample space for the back-up vehicle to park and lay out the picnic. Many of the picnic spots became as established as the route itself. A comforting familiarity often in the middle of a long, tiring hot day.

Meeting the crew at the picnic spot near Fron Farm 1990 (Photo courtesy of David Elliott)

Picnic spot near Fron Farm 1998. Judy, Nicola and Ursula with the very kind chap who helped crew that year

After our refreshments we followed the drovers' route that left the tarmac to cross the beautiful open grassy paths towards Cwm Owen, also known as The Griffin Inn. We would canter along the grassy trail as the booming sounds coming from the firing range got louder. I remember the fear as we rode towards the sounds when all I wanted to do was ride away.

Cwm Owen
2019

Cwm Owen once provided food and rest for drovers and their cattle and later became a pub called The Griffin. It closed its doors to the public in 2001 and became a private dwelling. It is reported to have been a tavern as long as anybody can remember, with grazing for travelling droves. During the first half of the twentieth century it was a venue for pony sales. The Griffin, during our trekking years marked the approximate halfway mark of the complete route from Affcot Mill to Llangrannog. Half the distance - not necessarily half the time. Also only half the distance if the route was followed with no mistakes. It also marked the last bit of civilisation before we entered the military firing range marked with sinister scarlet flags. On the return trip The Griffin was a welcome sight, on the outward trip, leaving it behind filled me with fear.

Epynt comes from a Brythonic word meaning place of the horse. Brythonic was the Celtic language from which Welsh emerged. With mynydd being translated as mountain, we have "Mountain crossed by a Horse Path".

The permanently hoisted flag at the boundary of the military range, 2019

The scarp can be seen for miles upon miles from all directions. It is a huge brown massif bizarrely stippled with numerous small, geometric conifer plantations. I call them giant furry caterpillars; they distinguish the mountain from others in the Elenydd. The oversized critters make the plateau look strangely sinister. The upland has many stories weaved around its existence.

"Caterpillars" on the Epynt, 2019

I've gleaned the following information about the Epynt from a number of sources which are listed in the bibliography at the back of the book. "An Uprooted Community" by Herbert Hughes is a detailed and moving account of the people who lived on the Epynt and his book was intended to act as a lasting memorial to those who were displaced.

Mynydd Epynt is a vast upland area in Powys bounded by the valleys of the rivers Usk, Irfon and Wye. The plateau reaches 1558 ft above sea level at the top of Tri Chrugiaue.

The plateau is embedded with political controversy due the uprooting of a community with little compensation paid to the families who were forced to vacate in 1939. 219 men, women and children were compelled to vacate fifty four farms and holdings at short notice, without certainty of acquiring alternative homes.

The Ministry of Defence took over several thousand acres of Mynydd Epynt in 1939 and, being a training area with an artillery range, there has consequently been little access across the land since. The plateau is also known as SENTA – Sennybridge Training Area or Sennybridge Range. I shall refer to it as the Epynt as that is its historic, rightful name from when it was an inhabited upland area.

Of significant importance was that this disruption moved "Welsh Speaking Wales" from near Brecon to Carmarthenshire.

The rather scary memories of us crossing the Epynt in the 80's and 90's are insignificant in comparison to the trauma that those families went through during their removal and subsequent years during resettlement. Still now, I'm sure those still alive and their descendants must be deeply affected.

"Cofiwch Epynt" appeared on a banner on the A470 near Rhayader in April 2019. This is a nod to the many slogans painted throughout Wales in recent years reading "Cofiwch Dryweryn", which refer to the uprooted community and subsequent drowning of the village of Capel Celyn in 1965 to provide Liverpool with water.

Cilieni school was also within the seized zone and a plaque was erected in 1996 where its classrooms once stood. It has the names of the 16 children and teacher at the school when it was closed in 1940. Mrs Olwen Davies was there with the children on a Monday in September 1939 when an army captain broke the news of the closure to her in front of the children. By all accounts she was terribly distressed and the children wouldn't have understood as the captain spoke in English. She carried on with the lessons of the day as best she could, letting the parents tell the children later. The writing along the bottom of the plaque reads:

"No more fun and healthy play, without the small school the valley is empty".

There is a photo of those last pupils alongside their teacher, Mrs Olwen Davies, taken in 1996 at the site of the school. It can be seen within the pages of Herbert Hughes's book.

Memories told by residents are heart wrenching. Edna Williams was present when the army captain visited her father to notify him of the intentions. "What if we cannot find somewhere else to go?" her father asked. "Then you will be thrown out onto the road," the officer replied.

Ronald Davies, author of The Epynt Without People, describes the Winter of 1939 after they'd received the news:

> "Winter soon set in, one of the coldest winters in living memory. The weather was cold and everyone's heart was stone cold at the thought of having to move and wondering where they could find another home.
>
> They wondered if it was worth doing any hedging, was it worth sowing basic slag, was it worth digging a gutter, was it worth repairing the roof of the barn? Many of the older folk I am sure were wondering if it was worth living anymore"

Following the sale of over two hundred cattle at a special auction in December, Ronald writes:

> "On May 21st, 1940, the War Office issued an order that all the ponies grazing on Epynt were to be removed by the 20th June at the latest, as firing would commence on the 1st July."

Today only sheep are allowed to be grazed on the Epynt and the farmers are aware of the risks. In the early years horses used to wander onto the range. There are tales of a stallion who repeatedly evaded capture. In 1954 a horse was spotted on the range and promptly shot.

How cruel the bitter irony of such actions to have been executed upon The Epynt -The Mountain of the Horse.

In June 1940 lorwerth Peate was asked by the Museum of Wales to carry out a final survey and take photographs. On his final visit he found *"unlocked doors, unadorned windows with the panes staring vacantly at me, a cat which had been left behind retreating nervously through a hole in the cowshed door, an occasional cow or heifer, which would be collected on a last visit, running confidently towards me on seeing a living being in that deadly silence which they could not understand."*

Peate passed the family from Hirllwyn *"with their load of furniture on a cart coming through the mountain gate"* He met a lady of eighty two who was expecting to leave later that day. *"She had dragged an old chair to the furthest end of the yard and was sitting there motionless, gazing towards the mountain with tears streaming down her cheeks".* She told Peate to get back to Cardiff as soon as he could, adding "it is the end of the world here".

Thomas Morgan from Glandwr used to slip back to his farm and light the fire to keep the house aired. One day he arrived to find his home in ruins. An army captain told him it had been blown up and he was not expected to come back again.

In 2010 a project to highlight the sacrifice of the residents of Epynt Mountain took place. A number of "children of Epynt", people born there now in their 70's, 80's and 90's, took part in a four mile walk in the area accompanied by members of the Brecknock Federation of Young Farmers Clubs.

The project also involved an award-winning play about the end of the community, written by Euros Lewis, which gathers together stories of those who once lived on Epynt.

Euros said:

> *"When this largely Welsh speaking community went in 1940 it was the death blow to Welsh speaking Breconshire".*

> *"It was said that this was not one community but a collection of disparate farms. However, that was not true, they all gathered at one chapel and if one farm was in trouble they laid down a white sheet on the hillside and others would ride to their aid. It was definitely a community.*

Tragically a lot of those who left who would have been middle-aged farmers died at relatively young ages. Whether it was the stress or just the uprooting no-one knows.

But certainly, according to what people have said, one farmer is said to have 'cried himself to death' after being forced to leave his family farm".

A website called abandonedcommunities.co.uk at time of writing, provides a great source of information and photos of the Epynt under military occupation. Within the website is a link to a set of photos taken by Tarquin Wilton-Jones in August 2010. The link is CavingUK.

Tarquin was in search of a specific waterfall and was given the opportunity to be taken on a guided tour of the military range. He was able not only to take photos of the wonderful hidden waterfall named Ysgir Fawr, but also the training ground. His photos include pictures of the uncanny and soulless German mock village known as the FIBUA village which was built in the late 80's during the Cold War.

FIBUA (fighting in built up areas) is situated on the hillside to the east of Cilieni Valley. Although our routes didn't pass this area it can be seen from a great distance, planted unnaturally high unlike the Welsh communities which were always nestled lower down away from the harshest winter elements. Its church spire reaches into the sky and its mock gravestones are all the same. Prayers, funerals and burials have never graced its walls and the stones are more likely to offer protection for soldiers in their simulated warfare.

A twisted irony is that Capel Y Babell is now left in ruins. The original chapel is within the military zone. On occasion access is permitted for people to visit the graves. The chapel tumbled down and foundations are all that remain. Gravestones lean, moss-covered with grass and shrubs tangle their way across the tombstones.

After 1940 Rhys Price would go back to tend the cemetery at the chapel, lay flowers on the graves and trim the hedges. Travelling by bicycle he would carry a scythe and enough food to last the day. At a later date the army provided transport for him, and he continued to perform his duties until 1985 when he was 82.

A plaque found at the chapel site bears the quotation

".... And they shall beat their swords into plowshares, and their spears into pruninghooks: nation shall not lift up sword against nation, neither shall they learn war ay more" Isaiah Chapter 2 Verse 4

With all the deeply saddening tales of the people of the Epynt I feel the need to give examples of their way of life and hardy character. To cherish and remember their significance as an integrated part of mid Wales.

Being an important convergence for the Welsh drovers on their travels to the east, the Epynt community were an integral point of the annual event. Whilst droving their own sheep and cattle across the plateau, they would also provide services to the long distance drovers. Llandulas (now known as Tirabad) was where a certain Rhys Williams worked in the shoeing meadow making cattle cues and false coins which he sold to the drovers.

Children would run to the hilltops when they heard the commotion and the noise of the huge herds coming. There would be festivities with the arrival of the droves and boxing matches would be arranged between farmers and drovers and touring fiddlers would add to the merriment.

The people of the Epynt provided hostelries for the passing drovers and their cattle. The Cross Inn – now a ruin beneath the forest - was near to the shoeing station, the Spite Inn a little lower down the valley. Cwm Owen (The Griffin) is located on the eastern side of the plateau with the Drovers Arms taking a more central position. The Drovers Arms (Pen-y-Gefnfford) is now part of SENTA, and the soldiers keep it looking eerily real and life like. With windows and pub sign swinging, from a distance it might seem inviting only to deceive you with its hollow interior.

It would have been inviting when still in the hands of the landlady, Mrs Caroline Evans and her son, Jack Evans prior to 1940. At one time it was a bustling place, with maybe hundreds of cattle grazing and fertilising the halfpenny green at a time.

The communities grew wheat and oats using horses to plough and hand tools to sow, reap and harvest. Farmsteads would join forces to work on the harvests and rushes would be cut to roof the ricks, in which the harvest would be stored.

Of course, there were many shepherds who tended the sheep, whose milk was used to make rich cheeses and butter to sell at the markets. Their fleece was used to spin wool and to make thick warm socks, especially for the drovers. The farms were hives for the knitting, weaving and spinning industry.

Each farm would also have a peat bank where sods of peat were dried to be used as fuel. Rees Price, who was born in a homestead on the Epynt in 1874, took part in a number of interviews in 1959. In one such transcript he claims that his father and neighbour, on one occasion, found old swords in the depths of the peat bog.

Food such as gruel, cawl and oatcakes were staples alongside the meat and milk from their animals. Rendered fat would be used for tallow, for making candles. Lower leg bones would be boiled down to make oil which was good for the joints.

Pancakes, potatoes, eggs and bread were also favourites and buttermilk was a preferred drink due to the rarity of tea.

If Mynydd Epynt today appears bleak, dull and unwelcoming then rest assured it would have been a very different place when populated, however sparsely so. Indeed, the distance between the homesteads would have surely called for much hospitality and sharing. If you were to meet a neighbour from the next valley upon a hill, you would likely stop and chat. This is in strange contrast to big cities, where we can be living in each other's pockets yet never really communicate and as a result feel desperately alone.

Take the London Underground, hardly a word spoken. Not all people of the city are like this of course, townships can be lively, buzzing integrated communities as can remote mountains, in their own ways. I wish I could have ridden across the Epynt with its people still there. How would they be farming today I wonder? I'm sure there would be a quad bike or two!

They may have even helped us avoid the mires with their trails of broken white crockery marking the safest route, like they used to in the past.

Maybe we would have lodged at the Drovers Arms in the centre of the mountain, grazing our horses on the halfpenny pastures used by the cattle drovers in bygone days. We would at least have stopped to picnic somewhere on the top, admiring the spectacular view, upon the mountain of the horse path.

As a child I had no idea of the Epynt's history. I never even heard it mentioned, therefore I question whether any of the adults knew either. What we all knew about quite clearly though, was the military presence.

Jim Perrin, the award winning mountaineer and travel writer describes the Epynt in 1996:

> *"But you cannot walk freely along the crest of that scarp. From the brown moors above where Bronze Age man made his burial mounds, among which he placed the mysterious permutations of his stone circles, there comes the thud of howitzer shells, the stutter of automatic weapons, the ragged staccato of rifle fire.*
>
> *There are rights-of-way, of course, used since prehistory, and you may still use them 'by the book'. The battle-range ordinances tell you that you may pass here when the red flags are not flying. That's a sour joke. The knots of their lanyards are sealed with moss and algae, the gates' hinges rusted shut. These scarlet prohibitions are never taken down. For the public good, no doubt, but maintained by dishonesty and sleight of hand."*

The visitor centre for the Epynt Way. There was plenty of information inside and a heater blowing out hot air. It had a strange feeling to it. I wonder whether it was built upon an old farm or homestead. 2019

Today you can follow the Epynt Way on horseback, bicycle or by foot. It is a permissive bridle path that encircles the Sennybridge Training Area. 80 km in distance, it also has five "Receptor points" which provide shelter, a corral and parking for horseboxes. In addition there is now a visitor centre located on the B4519 between Upper Chapel and Llangammarch Wells.

Having reflected on the significance of the Epynt, as a location and a culture both in history and in the present day, I'll now get back into the saddle, for the crossing of the SENTA northern boundary into the danger zone and on towards Carmarthenshire.

Charlie on Zac, Kate on Gilly, Wendy on Lewis and Beth on Hercules (1999)

Then we reached THE boundary. The northern boundary of SENTA (Sennybridge Training Area) or Sennybridge Range as I always knew it. For years those words alone terrified me.

I wonder if the military always knew we were there, I believe phone calls were made by our driver of the day in the morning, to which a mixed response would be relayed back along the crackling phoneline. We were never asked to leave the area but there was always a feeling amongst us that we were in danger and should have heeded the warning of the scarlet flags which were always flying.

The back-up Land Rover at the boundary in 1999. The driver of the day would meet the riders a last time before they left the public road to join a military road across the vast upland

Once our dedicated driver was asked to call the MOD and to inform them we would be crossing that day. When they sternly told our caller that we can by no means cross the range our driver merely told the truth, which was that we'd already entered the firing range.

Another account was that after our caller told the MOD the trekkers were crossing, the money in the phone box run out.

"Ride for your life! We're not supposed to be here!" was another reported quote.

We galloped where we could. Steph on Mandela, Charlie on Harvey and Nicola on Jack, 1998

Close up to an Epynt "Caterpillar" in 2019

There would be bullets clinking around the horses' hooves as we trotted along the bland, military roads, metal upon metal. The shoe of a horse, created to optimise our use of the animal for our leisure, pleasure and to work for us, and the metal bullets ricocheting off the hoof, created to kill a man.

Those same shiny bullets that Timmy, not even 10 years old, picked up and admired as the sun lit them up in his little hands. I don't think any got stashed into the saddle bags to play with later when bored at the hostel, that may have just been in my imagination.

As a child I was frightened by the terrifying boom of explosions, which nothing on a movie can match, however many speakers you surround yourself with. I was also appalled at the broken sheep we would ride past, blown to pieces in craters. A mess of rotten wool and bleached bones. I always rode with a deep sense of fear.

The Drovers Arms was the only other real landmark of consequence when we crossed the Epynt at the northern end. I was always excited to see a building, amongst the sound of explosions; it looked comforting from a distance, only to reveal itself as a spooky heartless empty void of a building.

There were also toilets on the range which we used when needed as the crossing could take a few hours. Little buildings with rooves and a seat under which was a never-ending abyss. You could not see the bottom, just a huge black void and I truly hope they were actually toilets and not some sort of military training tunnel system!

On one crossing I saw a soldier in the ditch, no more than 10 foot away. Lying on his belly, perfectly motionless. Camouflaged so effectively that all the riders ahead had ridden past him oblivious.

I called out to mum to alert her. "We can see you!" she mocked laughing, comforting me at the time with her light-hearted attitude. Only on reflection do I feel relief that the soldiers had actually seen US and used us as part of their training scenario.

No problem though, because one of our rider's friend was in the military and reassured her once that in August it would be the SAS training, therefore we were unlikely to be "shot by mistake".

Rachael (with her rather wicked humour) once told Steph and Charlotte that the red marks on the backs of the grazing sheep were actually crosses and were target practice for the soldiers.

I've since read that shells used on the range can have an 180m kill zone. How many broken and unexploded shells are on that range I wonder? In those early years when we strived to take the bridleways across the open hillside and struggled through the hideous bogs, we were surely lucky not to have stepped upon live ammunition. I shudder to think.

I recall during the early years of crossing the range seeing stark, fake buildings heartless and lifeless. As well as the FIBUA village, there are other target buildings dotted over the moorland and some of the dear little Welsh homesteads have been crudely rendered, grey, barren and colourless and used for sinister war exercises.

My research of the FIBUA mock village led me to some photos which, when I saw them, an overwhelming and haunting feeling of familiarity rose like an asp in my stomach. I'd seen it before, from upon my horse.

Because the German village is located on the East side of the Cilieni Valley, and with only our old, marked maps to look at it became clear to me how much we must have wandered off track.

Memories of the Epynt from all the people who rode with us in the mid 80's are hazy and it "all looked the same" up there. The routes across military-seized earth trodden by our horses' hooves in the early treks remain a mystery.

The moorland mires are a most fearsome memory of mine, together with crossing the military firing range. They came hand in hand. Not only did I suspect my beautiful horse and I may be blown to pieces, but it might happen whilst we sunk into the irretrievable depths of a bog. The bogs had our horses staggering wildly trying to pull themselves out. The dark blackish brown peat that splattered over the saddles and our clothes only revealed itself after the horses had already put their hooves on that perfect light green surface with its hidden peril.

From the Drovers Arms, during the early crossings amidst the boom of exploding shells, we ventured westward over Drum Ddu along the 'bridleway' towards Ffynon Dafydd-Bevan. Had we been more proficient with reading maps, we may have spotted how the route laced its way between the springs at the top of the valleys.

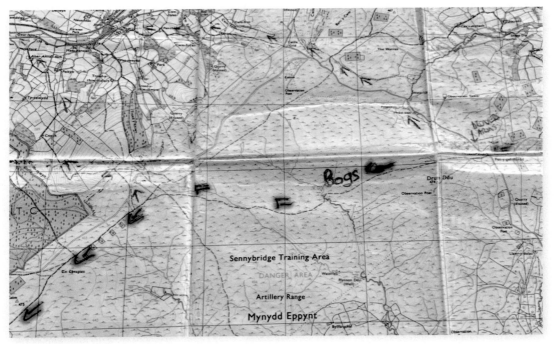

The many small tributaries that converged to form Ysgir Fawr, Ysgir Fechan and Nant Bran would likely have formed that blanket bog which we came upon, especially if we crossed slightly down the valley in the absence of a visible bridleway. The smudged ink tells the tale.   © Ordnance Survey 2021

Shouts from the front... "Bog" became all too recurrent and those atop the heavier ponies such as the cobs and hunters wished they were on the dainty Arabs and Section A mountain ponies. Each rider had to decide whether to follow the doom of the rider in front or pick their own route which could be safer, or much worse. I had memories of the lightest horses and riders being sent out first to test the ground. I then thought perhaps I'd imagined it, surely the kids weren't used as guinea pigs? Then I saw Tim's journal. Aged 11, he wrote freely; "We went over some boggy patches where Bosun and Ruth went into a bog. Me and Holly went first because we were the lightest and we led the way through safely".

Many ponies ended up belly-deep as they picked their way across the moorland. I would feel Lassie hasten her step as she dragged her hind legs desperately trying to defy gravity. I'll never ever forget the feeling of a horse sinking under the saddle. The floundering, the terror and the squelching gloopy noises as the bog sucked at the animal's legs like a monster.

As we rode on, looking back all we would see were pools of quivering chocolaty liquid where each hoof had tried to take hold. The peat would take several attempts to clean off where it had been slathered over the horses' silky coats and our tack. The consistency and colour were foreign to me as a child who lived in south Shropshire where the soil was grey-blue clay and although we had plenty of deep mud, it was always quite obvious and not hidden by an emerald green carpet of flora.

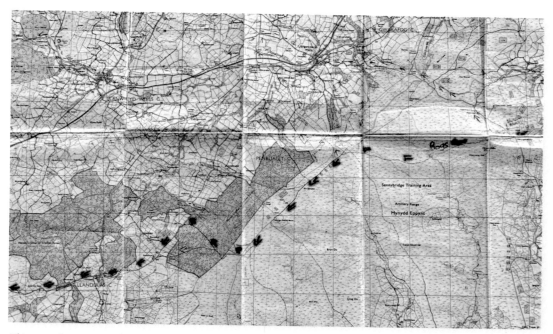

This map shows our earlier routes to Tirabad. It was possibly during these wanderings that we caught sight of the mock German village known as FIBUA. In the later years we simply followed the military road into Llangammarch Wells from the Drovers Arms
© Ordnance Survey 2021

We continued past Ffynnon Dafydd Bevan. Near the house was a well where the drovers' cattle would have drunk their fill on their way to Tirymynydd or the Drovers' Arms.

Writings by Sir John Lloyd in 1912 give further testimony to the land we tried to cross.

"The name on the Ordnance Map is Ffynnon David Bevan, or the well of David Bevan, and when I knew the place, a strong old man by name David Bevan, bordering on seventy years of age, lived there, and acted with his son and grandsons as the common shepherds of the stock on the waste land nearby.... At the time, about 1860, I was constantly going over to Llanwrtyd from Dinas, Brecon, to superintend the various improvements that were in progress.... Like the new road to Abergwessin, the restoration of the old parish church, and the building of a new school, and smaller matters like a sawmill...

Usually I left home (Dinas) at 2.00pm and allowed three hours to do the estimated nineteen miles so as to catch the night, as the saying is. One afternoon when I had gained the brow of the Ysgir farm, Coedcae, I found a thick mist had crept over the table land above, between me and the cattle track... I judged the course as well as I could, but made some mistake, and at last found my cob mare girth deep embedded in a black, soft bog. All in vain I urged the mare to try to struggle out; there she stuck without moving, sullen, and evidently terrified beyond measure. Night was almost on us. What was to be done! I bethought me of old Davy and resolved to proceed on foot to his cottage to seek his help. I somehow felt that it was unkind to leave the animal there alone.

It was however the right course to take. I soon found Ffynnon David Bevan, and amid a wondering group of the old man, the son and boys of all ages, including the son's wife, I told the story, and where my horse was fixed in the bog. Old Davy and his son knew the place well and told me not to trouble, but that if I could make my way on foot to Dolycoed, some five mile distant, they would bring my horse there almost as soon as I was! They made light of the matter as an everyday occurrence, and surely enough, we had hardly finished dinner when there was a clattering of hooves outside, and my horse was safely returned to its owner, not an atom the worse for what had befallen her.

It appears the whole family went out to the well-known pitfall bog; some took fern, some cut rushes, which they placed under the raised forefeet of the animal, making a firm foothold, and then some at the head and some at the tail, with a long pull and a strong pull and a pull all together, the mare took courage and made a grand effort, and out she came on to terra firma."

There is little remaining of Ffynnon Dafydd Bevan now, but it is surrounded by a cluster of trees which can be seen from a distance due to its high location.

South of the well and at the head of the Nant Bran, is a Bronze Age stone circle and cairn known as Ynys-hir. In 1940, before shelling destroyed the evidence, a careful archaeological dig took place. Two cremated burials , each in a small pit dug into the original surface of the ground, were found. One contained the bones of a young woman, the charred remains of her clothing, a pygmy cup and two beads, one made of pottery and another from anthracite.

Unaware of these ancient relics, we rode onwards to Tirabad, filthy, tired and keen to see people and civilisation that didn't include soldiers and tanks.

Prior to the forest commission building 25 houses, a school, a shop and a village hall for its employers in 1950, the village was simply Llandulas Farm, the church of St Davids, the Cross Inn and the Spite Inn, further down the valley. It was a meeting point for drovers travelling from different areas, providing lodgings before they crossed the plateau.

Legend tells that when Christianity first came to Wales an angel flew over the land with a bag of stones which were to be placed where churches would be built. As he flew over this desolate and remote place, a stone accidentally fell out of his bag and landed here, explaining why a church was built in such an inaccessible place. (irfonvalleyparish.co.uk)

After 1940 the congregation of St Davids church fell into single figures and by the end of the war it had fallen into disrepair.

Whilst the ride from Tirabad to Bryn Poeth Uchaf youth hostel in the earlier years went via Cynghordy with its magnificent viaduct, later treks saw us leaving the SENTA range at the north western boundary where we dropped steeply down into Llangammarch Wells and then on to Llanwrtyd Wells, a town which later provided our lodgings. Tim recalls in 1993 riding Cherry's horse across the range whilst she took a ride in the car as she felt unwell. Tim's pony Holly had suffered a few bites and a saddle rub the previous day, so she was unsaddled and bridled and left to run alongside the trekkers at her own free will. Holly would canter on ahead then circle back to find her buddy, Troy. That must have been a sight to see, a pony running freely on the "mountain of the horse path", with its history of many ponies living on its plateau before they were all removed in 1939.

Cloud inversion at Garth viewpoint situated on the road before leaving the military zone. Taken in 2019 with staccato rapid fire sounding in the background

Looking back over our ponies' tails at the Epynt we would see the formidable barren mass with its little rectangular caterpillar conifer plantations. Then we would look ahead between our ponies' ears and towards the coast. I tried to block out the inevitable return journey when we would encounter once again what had become a cold military plateau.

Taking refreshments after leaving the range at the northern boundary in 1990, with the "boiling Range Rover". The forecast was 95 degrees F (Photo courtesy of David Elliott)

Rosie and Jean riding Poppy and Lizzy. They are climbing onto the range during the homeward bound trek in 1988 (Photo courtesy of Jack Upsall)

Steph with Avalon, Rach on Mandela and Nicola with Jack in 1998 dropping down the steep scarp towards Llangammarch Wells. The horses were often tired after crossing the Epynt plateau and we would give their backs a rest and shake out our own legs on the grassy descent.

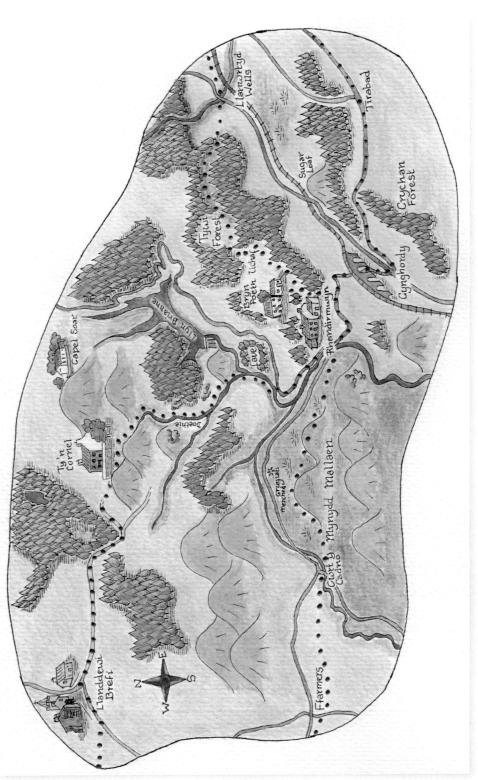

Map showing the initial route taken across Elenydd via the mires of Mynydd Mallaen and the preferred northerly route up the beautiful yet precipitous Doethie Valley

CHAPTER 8

Elenydd and Cwm Doethie

Down from the mountains and into civilisation we rode - to Llangammarch Wells. It is the smallest of four spa towns in mid wales, the others being Builth, Llanwrtyd and Llandrindod. The well in Llangammarch was known for its medicinal waters rich in barium but is now closed.

Llangammarch Horse Fair used to be the biggest pony fair in Wales and was famous throughout the British Isles. This changed when all the ponies were ordered to be removed from the Epynt by the Army in 1939-40.

Here follows excerpts from Llangammarch Past and Present – A history and Guide, written by John Pyper;

> *"Although little seems to have been recorded in print, it still brings back memories of Llangammarch's most exciting annual event to some local people.*
>
> *No doubt Llangammarch was a natural centre for a pony fair, lying at the foot of the Epynt, a mountain whose ancient names defines it as home of ponies.*
>
> *October 15th was the Fair Day unless it fell on a Sunday, when it would be on the Monday following.*
>
> *Very early on the day of the fair, ponies and horses would be driven from all over the Epynt, Upper Chapel and Llanfihangel Nant Bran, and from further afield, Abergwesyn and beyond.*
>
> *Horses would be streaming down by Penrhiw, Aberceiros, Troedrhiw, hundreds of them, before first light. Mrs Annabelle Thomas too, when a young girl at Cefn Farm, and*

not allowed to go to the fair, recalls the excitement of seeing the mass of ponies being driven past – "Wild little things, all different colours and so pretty."

Dealers would come from all over the country, many arriving on the mail train which reached Llangammarch station at 6am and then making for the Cammarch hotel for breakfast.

"There were no auctioneers – buyers and sellers would haggle and when a deal was struck would clap hands on it.

At the end of the day, there would be much celebration in the pubs and a big dinner was laid on in the Cammarch.

It seems that the fair survived through the last war and three or four years after it but with the removal of the ponies from the Epynt and the swift invasion of tractors to replace the working horses it was fading fast. By the last years of the 1940's it had disappeared, to be succeeded by the auction sales of ponies at Cwm Owen and Llanafan".

The final miles of that fourth day in the saddle saw us cross the river Irfon at a ford near Llangammarch and then follow the river along the lanes to Llanwrtyd Wells. When we sacrificed our visits to Bryn Poeth Uchaf hostel due to the limited vehicular access, Llanwrtyd Wells and Ty' n Cornel hostel at the head of the Doethie Valley became our favoured lodgings.

In Llanwrtyd Wells we grazed our horses near the railway station which was a little way out of town, away from the hotel where our dinner and beds were waiting. I remember it being a particularly long walk and we used to fight between ourselves to catch a lift in the Land Rover, tussling to find a space amongst the grooming kits and saddles. Anything to rest our already tired legs and avoid walking on the tarmac. Most of us had to walk however unless we struck lucky and it just made us appreciate the hospitality of the Neuadd Arms even more.

The hotel is over 145 years old and has a traditional farmers' Bell Bar; its original servant bells are still in place. When we stayed there it also had a rather randy big black dog that would harass the riders, shoving its snout where it was most unwelcome!

Hilary, Alex and Judy with Munchie, Maz and Mandela in front of the Neuadd Arms in 1995. The hotel had an attic like a rabbit warren and was home to a randy dog

The Neuadd Arms harboured dormitory type rooms in the attic, which was like a hot and musty rabbit warren. There was a bed in every nook and cranny, with stairs getting narrower and steeper with each storey climbed. Following the long walk from the horses field, our tired limbs still had this final feat to conquer.

Kylee remembers going up and up, "Are we there yet?" as she ascended each storey after a tough day in the saddle. Just when you thought it was as narrow and as steep as regulations would permit, there would be another little creaky door revealing yet more.

Llanwrtyd Wells is claimed to be the smallest town in Britain; it has a population of about 850 people but it has an incredibly big personality. It hosts most unlikely sporting events. Situated in the very heart of mid Wales between the Brecon Beacons and the Cambrian mountains it was a spa town that drew people from far and wide to drink its healing waters. The well, known as Ffynnon Ddrewllyd, is translated as "Stinking Well" and so called because of its strong smell of hydrogen sulphide. The well is located somewhere at the site of

Dol-y-Coed Hotel, which is now home to Charcroft Electronics, a major present day employer.

Whilst I'm on a watery thread, Llanwrtyd Wells also hosts the world Bog Snorkelling Championships. Something in my teenage years drew me to spectate this event and it was just as you would imagine it. Trenches of chocolatey bog water and people wearing snorkels and flippers - being timed. The catch being that no swimming strokes are permitted, the race is executed by using flipper-power alone.

The Cambrian Woollen Mill is one of very few working woollen mills left still operating in Wales and was rebuilt in 1902 after being reduced to a shell by fire in 1889. It apparently contains evidence of 700 years of weaving history. It is situated just to the north of the town and is passed by the competitors of the famous Man V Horse Race; something Maz and I had a crack at in 1991 and Shally and I in 1992. Twice we were pipped to the post by Zoe Jennings on Hussar. Twice we missed out on the £500 purse taken home by the first horse and rider to cross the line. It was incredibly close and a lot of fun. Here is how it came about…..

The event started in 1980 when local landlord Gordon Green overheard a discussion between two men in his pub, the Neuadd Arms. One man suggested that over a significant distance across country, man was equal to any horse. Green decided that the challenge should be tested in full public view and organised the first event.

Gordon Green, to the right of the picture, watches the runners start the Man v Horse race 1991

The atmosphere was electric and the horses incredibly excited 1991

Maz and me in the lead before being hunted down by Zoe on Hussar in 1991. The mountain bikers joked about grabbing Maz's tail for a pull up the hills, however on the downhills the bikes tore past us with terrifying speed.

Maz and me in 1991

The race is about 22 miles in length, just short of marathon distance, and the prize money rose £1000 per year for the runner who managed to beat the first horse. The biker Tim Gould beat the first horse in 1989 by three minutes, and in 2004 Huw Lobb, running on foot, beat the first horse during the 25th Man v Horse race and he won £25,000. There has been controversy with the race throughout the years, route distances for each discipline, vet checks, timings and so forth, but it remains a concept that inspires people both locally and from further afield.

So it was this little town, a hub in the middle of Wales, where we bedded down on our fourth night into our adventure for many years, the life and soul of a mid-Wales party. A lively setting between sleepy Glascwm and a paraffin and moon-lit Ty'n Cornel.

In the early years after our boggy crossing of the Epynt when we eventually arrived at Tirabad, we made headway to Bryn Poeth hostel along the lanes past Spite Inn farm to Cynghordy, passing under its magnificently curved viaduct before heading north on the lanes to the youth hostel warden's house at Hafod y Pant, where we took a rest day before traversing the Elenydd.

Cynghordy Viaduct 2019. I remembered thinking as a child how small all the horses and riders looked by comparison

Cynghordy viaduct 2019

The Elenydd is an upland plateau within the Cambrian Mountains, source of the rivers Elan, Severn, Teifi, Towy and Wye. It is also a name given to a division of land in Medieval Wales which covered approximately the same area.

Wikipedia also tells us that the Elenydd SSSI covers 22,770ha and is important both for its earth science and biological interest. The latter of which includes breeding birds and blanket bog, which the trekkers became profoundly aware of.

Emily Chappell, the award-winning travel blogger and cyclist, spent her childhood in mid Wales and describes what the Elenydd means to her. She's cycled across many parts of the world solo and took part in the 300km bike Audax of which the Elenydd was the centrepiece.

> "*The very name held magic for me: el–EN–ith: pronounced with the harsh voiced fricative Welsh shares with other ancient languages like Icelandic, and for me evoking an era of druids and dragons and ancient kingdoms, when unmotorized transport and inhospitable locals rendered this tiny Peninsula even more inaccessible. What went on in the barren folds of its mountains was unknown to the outside world, only available through what its inhabitants bothered to share or record....*
>
> *....We rolled along farm tracks and ancient drovers roads by day, slept in draughty bothies by night, and regularly paused to admire the great sweeping views that lay before us – either down into valleys green with farmland and speckled with villages, if we were on the edge of the range, or across a vast rolling landscape of featureless grassland and far horizons, if we were in its interior...*"

With the general interpretation being that the Elenydd starts north of Mynydd Epynt and stretches up to Pumlumon Fawr, then I'm sure some of our riding adventures covered the best bit, namely the Doethie Valley. Being southerly to the vast reservoirs and majority of pine forests, maybe the southern reaches of the Elenydd offer more of a reflection of what true historic mid Wales was once like. We also attempted to cross Mynydd Mallaen a plateau south of Doethie but struggled with the treacherous mires once again.

The Doethie Valley to me epitomizes singing birds, gurgling streams, tussocky grass, rain, sunshine, tumble down cottages and farmsteads coated in moss with hidden stories. Stone walls, sheep, kites and buzzards, dippers and dragonflies.

Having travelled the mid-section of the Elenydd using the mountain road from Tregaron to Abergwesyn with my daughter from the comfort of a car, I must comment that I'd much prefer to embark on that journey on a rainy day with a picnic and flask than to visit a plastic play barn or similar. There was not another car for miles or a snippet of phone signal. Ribbons of road stretched ahead with my daughter sitting on my knee and a remoteness that meant when the warning light came on to say "coolant low" my nerves were rattled to say the least. It's hard to imagine Emily Chappell amid hundreds of other cyclists wearing their brightly coloured apparel; all the colour we saw that day was a lonely phone box, bang in the middle of nowhere. A splash of red in a vast tawny landscape.

A colour splash between Tregaron and Abergwesyn taken on road trip in 2019. Near to this junction is Blaen Camddwr – "head of the winding stream". The Camddwr continues southerly until it feeds into Llyn Brianne and becomes part of the Afon Tywi that flows through Rhandirmwyn, on to Llandovery and into the sea at Carmarthen Bay.

A ribbon laid across the land. The Tregaron – Abergwesyn mountain road. The road in the distance leads to the Devil's Staircase before dropping down between the steep sides of Abergwesyn valley into the village, 2019

My memories of crossing the more northerly section of the Elenydd by pony when I was a small child are of horses floundering in bogs. My second crossing was an unforgettable adventure of fun, hard graft and sunshine with my friend Israel on our mountain bikes more than 30 years later. Although reservoirs dominated our landscapes, it was still a wild and beautifully remote expanse of land. As we cycled around the plethora of the lakes' "tentacles", whose endless reaches made the miles many, I'm sure the crows guffawed at us as they flew overhead from A to B.

It felt quite surreal when we came upon an isolated farm and some Highland cows; quite a contrast to the native Welsh Blacks who would have historically grazed the uplands. Both breeds are some the oldest in Britain; they go back to pre-Roman times. The Welsh Blacks are now on the list of endangered native breeds in Wales.

Like many remote parts of Wales, the Elenydd makes me feel small and rather insignificant in the world, in a good and humbling way.

Judy describes the ride from Llanwrtyd Wells to Hafod y Pant and

This Highland cow greeted us whilst we were off-road cycling between Claerwen Reservoir and Ffair Rhos on the Elenydd in 2013

Bryn Poeth Uchaf, our destination in the earlier years:

> *"From Llangammarch Wells we rode along the four mile lane to Llanwrtyd Wells, then the bridleway up into the forest for the last six miles. Got lost here – so difficult with forestry tracks that continually change and get muddled with the original bridle tracks. Compass no use as the paths wind round and around in circles. Wasted half an hour and about three miles (seemed like half a day). Joan and I knackered (remember this was a 40 mile day!) – I almost fell asleep in the saddle – I think the pressure of weeks of organizing myself and my family for this trek took its toll that hour."*

Tim's journal of the trek in 1993 when he was aged 11 years, reaffirms this tricky section of plantation "A new logging road had been made in the forest which confused us and we took a wrong turn and went 2 miles out of our way."

It was quite a different state of affairs in 2000 when this forest became a racetrack as Beau, a thoroughbred ridden by Karen and

Mandela our Anglo-Arab endurance horse ridden by myself, went flat out neck to neck. We didn't care which way we were heading, only which horse would tire first. Beau had the initial speed but Mandela had the stamina.

Judy continues:

> "The children were tired. Emily and James swapped ponies to give us a laugh. Em's long legs hung down on fell pony Velvet's fetlocks and James' legs barely went halfway down Maz (the tall American Saddlebred). But then Shally got his second wind and started to do that extended Arab trot with his feet flying forward in that showy, exaggerated fashion, so I had to wake up."

After the rather tedious forestry tracks from Llanwrtyd Wells through the southern section of Irfon Forest, we would come upon a little gem of a Welsh ruin. Its name was unknown to us during the many years we paused in its overgrown garden. Reached only by a long rough track it was remote and beautifully unspoilt. With a stream running in front of the old farm and outbuildings falling into disrepair, Judy would always comment that if there was ever another place she would like to live in, other than her beloved Affcot Mill, then this would be it.

Judy, Mandela, Cassie and Holly in 1999. Behind them is Cynnant Farm which was derelict for the many years that we rode past.

Cynnant Farm appears on the welshruins.co.uk website where Paul White exhibits his stunning black and white photography. Amongst the comments a lady who moved from Ascot to live there when she married the owners' son, recalled once being snowed in for a whole month and having to take the horse over the mountain track to Rhandirmwyn post office for food. Now 30 years later it has been renovated and is lived in again.

Cynnant Farm in 2019, having been restored

The lady who owned the cottage at the end of this bridleway took this photo by her lovely flowers – on the way to Bryn Poeth. Ros Field on the left riding Maz, joined the return trek homeward bound in 1989.

Swapping horses would lift our spirits when we were tired, a novelty and a lot of fun. Above in 1989 Judy is aboard Joyce's Troy, a handsome thoroughbred hunter type, next to Polly on Janie. Joyce and Celia are riding Shally and Maz

Joyce has a ride of Shalawi (Shally) Judy's purebred Arab and Celia tries out Maz, Em's American Saddlebred cross, 1989

Judy continues:

"Arrived at Bryn Poeth, the crofter's cottage in the mountains. Rode the ponies right up to the door, but no vehicle can get within ¼ mile. Ponies turned out around the cottage with two miles to roam, but they were never far and always came back at feed times. Sonny was very naughty at this place – he chased Timmy, bit another hosteller and kept coming in, even with a chair placed in the doorway. Once he walked right around the table.

No riding next day, two nights in the same hostel. Beautiful isolated cottage, no electricity, wood fire, gas lanterns. But this year NO WATER either. Oh well, kids, don't pull the chain when you wee, in fact don't wee!"

Whilst on the subject of peeing, I must add a nameless lady's recollection. Due to the water situation she decided to use the great outdoors for a pee and took two female friends to stand guard. To her horror some hostellers came upon the three of them and she hastily finished and whilst blushing, explained how she was looking for wild strawberries. She was aghast when the hostellers wanted to join her looking for the strawberries amongst the bracken.

And back to Judy's account - "Put used washing up water into the cisterns. Drinking water to be carried half a mile up from the farm in an assortment of bottles. (the top hot hill!) Other water collected from stream in deep gully outside hostel. O.K. really, once we are organised, just a shock at first.

Celia couldn't stand the harmonic snoring in the tiny, packed dorms and slept downstairs. [It really wasn't harmonic mother, you sounded like one of the wild boar from Treboeth]. Then the horses kept her awake tramping around the cottage on the only paving stones for miles. She swears they were my horses. Joyce missed her shower. Don't fuss girls, turn your knickers inside out! James is in a dorm full of girls and do they fuss him? It can't be maternal, he's too near their age. He laps it up. Kenchi not at all happy to be with the adults and

Timmy, doesn't stop saying "It's not fair!". In the end the girls make a bed for him in with them and he sneaks in with Rosie.

A lovely steak meal on our rest day. Slight bad feelings when we find the family in the annexe nicking the loo/washing up water that our strong, willing teenagers had carried up from the gully. Water worth more than money up here. In fact one chap went so far as to carry his water container everywhere with him – had it by him outside when he sat at the wooden table having his dinner – guarding it with his life! Nice lad though when we got to know him, an archaeologist. Couldn't understand why he wore a tie up at Bryn Poeth though. Celia became quite motherly towards him, giving him advice on cooking his meal – thought she was going to do it for him and offer to wash his smalls.

Cleaned tack on our day off. The wooden tables outside the hostel and the sunshine and the view made this a pleasant task. This is when some of us were so pleased to have our nylon bridles made by Sue (they convert easily into headcollars at picnic times). No leather to clean, just wash them. Later on too, they were a real advantage as we felt we could let the horses wear them in the sea. Went through tomorrows route with Joan. Even though she is driving she wants to know the way and may meet us and take photos."

The hill was grazed with sheep and rabbits alike and one self-sufficient lady hosteller caught, skinned and ate the latter. Becoming known to us as the "Rabbit Lady", I now envisage the rabbits being

nailed to the hostel door with string as occurred in the cult movie Withnail and I, "Here, Hare Here!"

Bryn Poeth Uchaf can be translated as "Highest hot hill" and opened as a hostel in 1969, providing a wonderfully basic, down to earth experience. A former farm bothy in the hills with no frills. The adjoining barn was later converted into a family annexe but sadly the hostel closed due to access difficulties in 1998.

Our horses were free to roam the hillside of many square miles but always stayed close by. Above they seek shade under the trees in which the hostel nestled on a scorching hot summer's day in 1990 (Photo courtesy of David Elliott)

Bryn Poeth Uchaf YHA. With no electricity, limited vehicular access and sometimes no running water, we still chose to take our rest day in this beautiful remote location near Rhandirmwyn. It closed in 1998 (Photo courtesy of Jane Osgathorp)

Rose with the three chestnut Arabs. Camille with the fly fringe was delivered to Affcot completely un-handled other than her transit to us. She was part of a semi wild herd of horses who needed to be found homes. It took a lot of time and patience to win her trust. With time she let us saddle and back her and she turned out to be a sweet gentle riding mare. She trekked to the coast as a four year old although she had a few shorter days, thanks to the presence of the trailer towed by David in 1990 (Photo courtesy of David Elliott)

Looking along the path, the only access to Bryn Poeth Uchaf Hostel. Our horses roamed the hillside freely. Lizzie poses in the sunlight (Photo courtesy David Elliott 1990)

The stream at the bottom of the bank at Bryn Poeth where we fetched our water when the hostel had no running water in 1989. Bob can be seen leading Sonny down for a drink. Judy and Sue T at the bottom next to Maz and I. Rosie halfway down

A mountain watering hole. Polly and Janie, like a fairy tale, they were such a perfect match. Rosie and Judy walk back up and Bob carries water up the hill for the hostellers, 1989

Above I was brushing off a saddle pad on our rest day at Bryn Poeth Uchaf with a little "help" from Tenpee (so called because he was won in a 10p raffle!). He was a cheeky little Welsh mountain pony perfectly at home in the Welsh hills. Another little native pony who came on some of the treks was Tinker. Both the little greys were notorious for bucking and they were passed around between many different riders to try and stop their antics. I think they mellowed naturally with age. David had managed to get the Range Rover near to the hostel that year and it can be seen in the background (Photo courtesy David Elliott 1990)

Maz thinks about coming into Bryn Poeth hostel in 1990 (Photo courtesy of Jane Osgathorp)

The resident sheep in front of the bunks at Bryn Poeth youth hostel in 1990 (Photo courtesy of Jane Osgathorp)

Judith prepares one of her famously garlicky spaghetti bologneses, this time at Bryn Poeth, 1990

The fond memories of Bryn Poeth Uchaf YHA are shared between the many of us who stayed there between 1985 and 1992. Louise who joined us in 1990 as a 12 year old, recalls the whole trek as one of her favourite experiences as a kid;

> *"I have many happy memories, swimming at the beach was wonderful with the horses and camping in a field of high grass and flowers with the horses all around. The most memorable place we stayed was the little cottage in the Welsh mountains which was small and quaint and we walked down the hill to the village for sweets and then had to trek back up."*

David also records in his journal;

> *"Trek Day 5 Rest day at Bryn Poeth. Another scorching day, most of it spent with Sue, Barry and Joseph in shady spot by the stream. The children walked over the hill and through the wood to the shop at Rhandirmwyn."*

Images of the Railway Children, Famous Five or even Hansel and Gretel come to mind where the children go into the woods and find sweets... without the witch thankfully. The excitement of a few hours without the grown-ups and a new place to explore created cherished memories.

Sometime after 1991 we sacrificed our visits to Bryn Poeth in favour of Ty'n Cornel, the latter having better vehicular access to bring to us our belongings after a long day in the saddle. Consider that we're not talking toothbrushes and PJ's, but horse feed and bowls, dog food and bowls, rugs, grooming kits, first aid kits, (human, dog and horse), our food plus twelve or so overnight bags, it made sense to bring the crew vehicle as close as possible and as I recall the dogs slept in the vehicle as most YHA's don't allow them inside.

A word about our trusty Land Rovers....

Alongside riding skills, the adults on the treks were required to take a turn driving. Sometimes in company, other times alone. Bearing in mind there were no mobile phones, the driver needed to find their way to the arranged picnic spot. Woe betide the driver who failed to bring the riders their lunch!

There is also an appendix in the back of the book detailing the "wheels" of the treks including some photos.

The first Landy in the Collyer household was a Series II J plate built in 1970. We travelled to pony club rallies sitting on the rear bench seats with saddles on our knees, bridles hanging off our ears and no doubt grooming kits wedged where the sun doesn't shine. Mother used to tow a double-length trailer that if packed carefully, would carry 5 small ponies. It was like a Tardis. She also used to save fuel by turning the engine off when we came to a downhill.

At some point during the 80's the Series II was replaced with a Series III K plate built in 1971, therefore pretty similar. This I believe is the one that finally blew up in Knighton in 1990 aged 19. Such was the force of mechanical failure that it sent Vivien's rather obnoxious Jack Russell flying forward into the front where it became wrapped around Barry's neck like a living stole. It was the same vehicle that Celia had been driving with Peggy and horsebox in tow, when she got ushered into the Royal Welsh show having got caught up in the show traffic at Builth Wells. Perhaps the marshals thought the LR was a vintage exhibit.

Around 1993 came the LR Defender D'OOP, built in 1986, an upgrade and reliable to a point. It was reported to have brakes less effective than desired and a sporadic reverse gear. Steph remembers negotiating country lanes one year without a reverse gear or a handbrake. However, we got a lot of stuff in it and it was great for the dogs to sleep in. For 9 years D'OOP faithfully served our treks before it was passed on.

In 1999 there was a significant upgrade when the back-up vehicle became a shiny ex-demo Discovery R'AUX, made in 1997. It didn't take long for it to be "worn in" with bite marks on the bonnet where the horses who had been tied to the bull bar had taken a liking to the taste of paint. A huge dent appeared in the rear wing where Judy had over-steered, only to be righted with a good hard donk from an adjacent bank. Not bothering with an insurance claim the dent stood proud, gently rusting away, on the rear off-side wing until R'AUX retired almost 20 years later. Baler string was always tied onto strategic points on the roof-rack, flapping in the wind as it traversed the Welsh countryside rammed with all things equine, canine and human. Seedlings would grow in its roof gutters where hay seeds had settled after visits to the farm where it was often stuffed full of hay bales in addition to the five bales routinely put on the roof rack and "secured" with a couple of bungees.

There were various other vehicles that joined us here and there. A pair of Range Rovers, one yellow and one blue, in 1990 both managed to negotiate the track up to Bryn Poeth Uchaf driven by David.

Just like some of the horses and riders had their ups and downs, so did the motors. Thurs 2nd August 1990 David's journal reads "The Range Rover kept boiling – very hot day – 95 degree forecast" whilst he made his way across Sennybridge firing range.

Catherine (Elliott) at the tack box. Often we took a trailer in case a horse went lame or had saddle sores. There would need to be a lot of shuffling around of gear for a horse to take a ride. (Photo courtesy of David Elliott, 1990

After the rearrangement of our digs, the ride from Glascwm to Llanwrtyd became much more manageable and the ride from Llanwrtyd to Ty'n Cornel, a mere trot up the valley! Provided we didn't succumb to bogs or canyons.

On our very first trek to Llangrannog we crossed the Elenydd via Mynydd Mallaen. An expansive plateau with a small population of hill farms breeding sheep. On its highest point are two Bronze Age cairns called Crugiau Merched, translated as Ladies' Barrows'

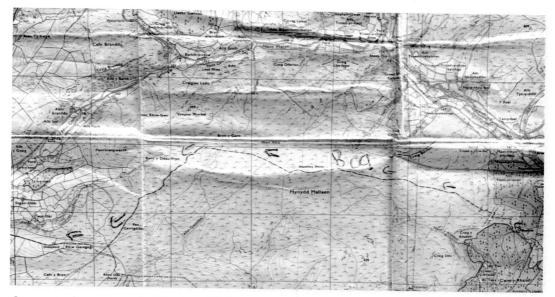

Once again the map is marked "bog" scribbled on top of arrows which had themselves bled, ink running as if the maps had been dropped amidst the chaos and panic. Above the arrows on the map are the Bronze Age cairns.

© Ordnance Survey 2021

Leaving the mires behind in those early years, we then made our way to the coast on the safety, albeit tedium, of tarmac. First to Cwrt y Cadno then Ffarmers, south of Lampeter on to Llanybyther and Pont Sian finally crossing the main coastal road at Plwmp to drop down to Llangrannog.

During the earlier years the horses were put to pasture at Llangybi, splitting the final trek into two parts. The distance from Bryn Poeth to Llangrannog is around 46 miles, provided there were no wrong turns and so would have been too brutal for the final day. So the riders would travel by car to Llangrannog and travel back the following morning to ride the last section. The farmer at Llangybi was very proud of his grey stallion and the children often had a sit on his bare back. I'm not entirely sure if the stallion was even broken in, but he seemed docile enough.

Travelling by Land Rover to our final destination without our trusty steeds however didn't quite feel right. We wanted to share the final descent with the horses as a team. A couple of years later the accommodation was jiggled to use Ty n Cornel hostel instead of Bryn Poeth. This was somewhat of a sacrifice as we loved Bryn Poeth so much, despite its inconveniences, and although this change made the

Catherine (Upsall) sitting upon the stallion at Llangybi in 1988 (Photo courtesy of Jack Upsall)

final day a rather tough 36 miles, it meant we all arrived at Llangrannog together. Details of all the distances between the overnight stops over the years as the route changed, can be found in Appendix 6.

Judy improved the route greatly when we started to ride up Doethie Valley from Rhandirmwyn rather than the mires of Mynydd Mallaen.

Rhandirmwyn pronounced "ran-dee-mo-n", can be translated as "valley of the minerals" due to the lead mining that took place in the Towy valley.

Situated in farmland near the village is the 600-700 year old

Judy, Charlie, Nic, Wendy, Beth and Kate stop for an ice-cream break in Rhandirmwyn before heading up the Doethie valley. The Royal Oak pub can be seen in the top left of the photo behind them. Horses from the left are Mandela (Great grandson of Chalice), Zac, Jack, Lewis, Hercules and Gilly 1999

Pwllpriddog Oak. Its girth has been measured at 28ft and being hollow, it reportedly once provided a hiding place for a king. The village pub being named The Royal Oak may pay testament to the story, and in 2018 the Woodland Trust awarded the oak "Tree of the Year". Aside from a king's concealment the tree has also been used as a pigsty, a duck roost, and has even had live music performed from within it

Rhandirmwyn is also well known for Twm Sion Cave. In an extract from Hawkmoor – The Adventures of Twm Sion Cati, Lynn Hughes tells us a little about the latter-day Robin Hood of Wales:

> *"Violence was the order of the day in 16ᵗʰ century Cardiganshire, the least law-abiding corner of Bloody Mary's kingdom. The mountains and valleys of Wales in those queer times harboured a gallery of rogues, but none more notorious than Twm. A two-sided character: highwayman, outlaw, scallywag on the one hand, poet, scholar, nobleman on the other, he charmed his way through adventures which still live on in popular imagination – in wild west Wales.*
>
> *In his skirmishes with the diabolical Vicar and the smooth-talking Sheriff, Twm Sion Cati is one man, but in his wooing of Johane Williams, the lovely Lady of Ystradffin, he is quite another."*

Above the confluence pool of the Pysgotwr and Towy rivers, Twm Sion Cati Cave is hidden in an RSPB nature reserve called Gwenffrwd Dinas. Twm was believed to use the cave to hide from the Sheriff of Carmarthenshire and it is accessed from the steep wooded slopes of what is now the reserve. The cave walls are covered in engravings and etchings from throughout time, some allegedly dating to the 1700's.

The conical hill is covered with majestic oak woods and became a reserve in the 1960's when it was home to a small number of Red Kites who were believed to be the only remaining breeding pairs in the whole of Britain. They were later successfully reintroduced to other parts of Wales and have since spread to England. During our treks we would see the Red Kites high above our heads and marvel at their splendour, unaccustomed to their shape, with their forked tails, quite different from the buzzards we were used to seeing from the east.

Dinas Reserve where Twn Sion Cati's cave can be found, 2019

Moss-covered boulders on the path to the cave in Dinas reserve, 2019

Llyn Brianne is reportedly the highest reservoir in Britain. On the map it looks like a wiry, gangling dragon with its wings held high. Misplaced. As if dropped from another world. When you are beside it, you feel very small. It is immense and magnificent. Stunning as she is, it saddens me to see the conifers ripped up along her banks. Harvested for timber and paper for our growing population, deep dark Gruffalo woods with barely a shaft of light able to penetrate its canopy and nothing can grow on the dark and acidic forest bed of needles.

The desecration at the side of the road by Llyn Brianne 2019

Llyn Brianne Reservoir, the creation of which caused much protest, 2019

Nicola, Tracey, Kate and Beth using an alternative route to avoid the precipitous Doethie Valley descent. Pictured in front of part of the Llyn Brianne reservoir 1999

Reservoirs and conifer plantations have transformed so much of Wales. Where there would once be small settlements and farms, communities of many generations with their churches and schools, now lie huge glistening lakes and black forests.

Many old drovers' routes have been lost under the lakes and forests but some still remain. Now, the long, narrow, winding metalled roads like ribbons are lain across the moors, and woodlands, and follow the perimeter of the lakes. I imagine the water seeping like black ink into the folds and crevices of the land when the dams were finally completed and the valleys were immersed. A habitat changed forever.

"Often referred to as drowned villages, in times of drought the buildings can be seen peeking out of the water. From the bed of Lyn Brianne, Fanog farm has emerged eerily from its watery grave. Word got around and soon there were hundreds of visitors climbing all over the old ruin. And yes some wag put a, 'For Sale,' sign on it. There were no takers, apparently it only had a short lease." (rhandirmwyn.net)

There was much opposition to the building of the Lyn Brianne reservoir including William and Jane Jones, they were brother and sister and they fought tooth and nail. Although they and the other objectors managed to stop a construction road from being built through Doethie valley, it seems the authorities were always going to build the dam. The Jones' died before the dam was built.

Jim Perrin the British mountaineering and outdoor writer, on his way to Doethie Valley writes about Llyn Brianne;

"It's reached from Rhandirmwyn by walking up towards the new reservoir of Llyn Brianne, the disfigured hand-shape of which grasped too much of Wales' beauty when it drowned the infant streams of Camddwr and Craflwyn, Tywi and Nant Gwrach. Those culpable surveyors looked, no doubt, at the adjacent valleys of the Doethie and the Pysgotwr, and I don't for a moment disbelieve that they are capable of looking there again (at Blaen Doethie currently there are plans to install a huge wind-farm development, which would be desecration here)"(The Hills Of Wales)

Ystradffin at time of writing was under construction with the creation of a hydroelectric scheme to use water from Afon Towy for power using two huge turbines. As I passed the site there were fields of pipework, which you could drive a small car through. There was also a brightly coloured alien crane, like a praying mantis, and construction traffic crawling through the beautiful valley. Apparently the scheme had to be resubmitted to avoid the most environmentally sensitive area. Nonetheless protestors, especially anglers, I'm sure are right to be concerned. The local farm was soon put up for sale.

The Capel Celyn flooding, north west of Bala in Wales, was the most protested reservoir project which is why you will see 'Cofiwch Dryweryn' painted on many rocks and walls throughout the country. 'Remember Dryweryn'.

After an original graffiti was destroyed in Aberystwyth and replaced with 'ELVIS" these remembrances were painted throughout Wales in response. There were more than 50 at time of writing.

This wall is in Llangrannog. There was also a protest graffiti at Tresaith, and many more were appearing in 2019

With Rhandirmwyn and its surroundings having had more than its fair share of damaging developments and proposals, let us thank those who protested with all their heart against a construction road being gouged through the Doethie Valley.

We would then begin the meander up one of the Elenydd's true treasures. Doethie Valley is silver with bubbles and spray, as if a big-hearted mythical giant sat at the head of the valley and popped open a bottle of the finest champagne, pouring it gently into the valley with a hearty smile.

Doethie Valley 2019

The paths are rich with sounds, sights and scents. The valley also has hidden perils especially for those upon a horse. A postcard of Doethie Valley sent home in 1998

The riders taking a break in the Doethie Valley in 1988. From left to right, Rosie riding Bronwen, Janie, Kenchi riding Filly and myself riding Sandy. Judy on foot and an unidentified bottom on the right

The path up Doethie Valley at times was reduced to a slippery, rocky outcrop like the one above near Cnwch Craig Glas. This proved dangerous for the horses to negotiate (2019)

Jim Perrin describes this jewel in the heart of Wales:

"There are many places in Wales of which I am fond, all of them entrancing in their different ways and at their proper seasons. But if I were asked by a stranger to this loveliest of all countries which place is the most beautiful, then I would tell of the pleasure in walking up the Afon Doethie on a fine day in the high spring of May or June when hawthorn blossom beacons the hillsides and bluebells shimmer like a low flame amongst the wood"(Travels With The Flea)

From within his 2016 publication "The Hill of Wales" we can once again imagine walking with Jim:

> "There is an excitement about this valley of the Doethie. It plays on your anticipation. You see just so far into it, and then a bend obscures, a craggy bluff juts out above the stream and you follow ledges above the falls and pools, the mountain ash, the holly and the small, twisted oaks that cling to their riparian steeps. Beyond there is the haven to which your curiosity has led: a bushing of sweet ash and oak woodland between these valley thighs, distance too in the sight, that takes beauty beyond its admirers; and there is old memory – in the broken-down walls of those who lived here in the summer pastures of years ago."

With its beauty though came danger. Like a Belladonna flower… pretty as can be but toxic if eaten, the valley has hidden perils. The path can be narrow and very precipitous. With horses being somewhat unpredictable in nature there were many close calls. Many of us jumped off the horses; as much as we loved our furry friends, we weren't ready to join them into the depths of the valley should one of their four feet slip, ending in disaster. It was terrifying.

Nicola was seen holding desperately on to Jack's reins from the ground whilst he pirouetted on a knife-edge cliff. Wendy remembers seeing walkers approach with flapping cagoules, the inevitable "spooker" for horses young or old. Luckily she jumped off before Lewis saw them, before he scrambled around in fright, teetering on the edge kicking stones down far, far below into the ravine.

Many times we tried to find an alternative route around Craig Cnwch Glas, the most notorious section, but detours always led us into bogs. Such detours once ended up in the riders getting totally lost and arriving at the hostel at 10pm, shattered, cold and hungry, as Alison Hall recalls

In the late 90's after too many close calls with horses not as sure footed as Mandela (aka a mountain goat), Nicola created an alternative route from Rhandirmwyn to Ty'n Cornel which some of the riders chose to take instead. Kenchi still shivers with fear when you mention his experience of riding up the Doethie Valley in 1989. Judy recounts:

"A beautiful ride today down to Rhandirmwyn, then alongside the river Towey, crossing it twice then the river branches left and becomes the river Doethie, and up the remote Doethie Valley – no road for miles, only a rather precarious bridle path, especially the bit around Cnwch Glas rock. Oh my God, glad I didn't see Kenchi and Velvet's antics. I was in front and just heard a bit of fuss behind. Celia told me later that when Velvet was scrabbling around the rock with the stream far below, and just when she needed her head, Kenchi pulled the reins and sort of leaned back as she was fighting to go forward. Her back legs were dangerously near the edge, her front legs pawing the air, trying to regain her foothold on the rocks. "Kenchi hold her mane, let go of the reins" Celia called out urgently to him. (Kenchi would have been just 10 years old and terrified!). Joyce got off, calmed Kenchi down and led Velvet then from Troy. Next minute all was forgotten and he was singing to Velvet, but Celia and Joyce were shaken, glad I didn't see it. Going back we'll lead them around that rock.

You have to make sure you keep to the path up this valley as it is boggy in parts – once or twice we took the wrong "path" and ended up in a boggy bit. The faster you go over the bogs the better, but I am a baby and got off at any suspicion of a bog and ran across leading Shally. Poor Celia and Nutmeg had difficulties. Nutmeg got into a bog up to her belly but managed to scramble out! You are brave Celia, staying on board.

Lovely valley, you never know what's around the next bend. Curlews, red kites, buzzards. You get the unreal feeling that the word "pollution" is just a myth and the expressions like "greenhouse effect" and "dead rivers" must be terms used by pessimists. When you see that clear, busy, gurgling little stream below, the blue sky above and the mountains around and your horse is fit and loving every minute of this adventure, you just feel the world is perfect and untainted."

Wendy, Kate and Beth pause for a breather on the Elenydd riding Lewis, Gilly and Hercules (1999)

Near Ty n Cornel on a summer's day in 1994. From the left, Rachael on Star, Judy riding Shally, Alison on Paddy (aged just 4), Julia on Maz and Emma riding Selina.

The valley path leads right to the doorstep of Ty' n Cornel Hostel. When we visited it was owned by the YHA and had no electricity. It is still the most remote hostel in Wales but has since had improvements made to it, including electricity supplemented by solar energy and a log burning stove. It is now owned and run independently by the Elenydd

Wilderness Hostel Trust, a charity created in 2006 when the YHA announced it was to sell Ty n Cornel and Dolgoch. The latter is 6 miles easterly across the hills and sits in the conifer plantations north of Lyn Brianne reservoir.

The journey to Ty'n Cornel was also a challenge for the one whose duty it was to drive the Land Rover that day. From Rhandirmwyn they drove up to Soar Y mynydd chapel and across a stony track to the hostel. It was the old drovers' route except in reverse when followed on the outward bound trek.

An extract from a postcard sent to Rosie from Judy in 2000 tells the tale:

> *"Em and Charlotte went up the Doethie Valley yesterday (round Cwnch Glas rock where Kenchi and Velvet went backwards). The other two were chicken and went around the top, as did the Land Rover and me up an incredibly steep, stony track. Low ratio gears essential, quite scary as it was virtually climbing a mountainside in a vehicle. Once you started there was no going back, but we did it and saw Em, Charlotte, Zach and Mandela and two dogs as tiny specs far below. It saves 25 miles going around by Tregaron to get to Ty'n Cornel. Charlotte has driven off-road bits – you can do it next year! Love Mother"*

Ty' n Cornel can be translated as "the house on the corner" and is a 19th century converted farmhouse.

It evokes for me memories of midges, heavy mists, silence... and more midges!

Its stillness and tranquillity was perhaps intensified because we'd been following first the Afon Tywi and then the Doethie for eight miles up the valley, the chattering stream at first flooding our senses but then as the miles went by, eventually becoming a part of us, much as if you live by a railway you become accustomed to the trains and hardly notice their passing.

The twilight silence at Ty' n Cornel would only be broken by the ferocious snoring from the dorm causing mattresses to be strewn in corridors and corners!

Half-light envelopes the edges of the Elenydd for many hours in summertime. A far cry from how it might look in the depths of winter when I imagine further down the valley the Doethie stream would be half frozen with icicles, and glistening ice would cling to the rocks and provide no grip for a horses hoof.

In the summertime hostel though, souls would be heaped under blankets scattered around the house, dreaming of journeys and adventures, maybe dreaming of home or perhaps of the sound of the seashore becoming ever closer.

The setting was not particularly pretty after the valley, unlike Bryn Poeth Uchaf, there are no trees. Exposed and functional, it was gratefully received by us and no doubt many before us and after us. It provided shelter and facilities.

Such was the exposure at the head of the Doethie that we often rugged the horses. The first year we visited we were ill prepared and it was noted that blankets from the beds were used. They were of course put back on the beds in the morning, with a slightly horsey aroma to them. Those old grey and brown blankets the hostels used to provide were very different from what you see in hostels now. It would be far too conspicuous to throw a duvet over the horses hind quarters with their brightly coloured covers these days.

A well-earned rest day for the herd, 1999

Sleepy horses at sunrise 2000

Ruth and Jess near Ty' n Cornel 1994

Ruth and Jess sharing a beautiful view, 1994

Charlie on Harvey, Rach on Avalon, Nicola on Jack, Judy on Mandela and Steph on driving duty with Holly. In front of Ty'n Cornel YHA, ready to set off on the final day's ride to the sea in 1998

Beau and Mooney. Best friends. Up high on the Elenydd, we often put rugs on the horses to protect them from the midges and the weather even in July (2000)

Kizzy and Charlotte relax at Ty n Cornel after a long day, 2000. Kizzy was always rather spoiled!

Rachel B recalls a night at Ty' n Cornel;

"Probably the funniest memory I have is at Ty' n Cornel when another man staying there told us ghost stories. As there was no electricity we had to go to the loo in the dark with a torch. The only one that worked was Alison's amber roadside lamp so we sat on the loo to flashing indicators!"

In 2000 Tracey remembers how impressed we all were when Karen produced a magnum bottle of Champagne at Ty' n Cornel. There we were, high up in the Elenydd wilderness sipping Champagne. We've no idea how she kept it hidden for so long or how it remained uncorked at Bleddfa.

Across the hill a couple of miles from the hostel is Soar y mynydd, the most remote chapel in Wales. It is a grade II listed building made of local rubble stone collected from riverbeds and ruined farmsteads in the area. It has a beautiful simplicity about it, tucked in amongst trees; a simple whitewashed rectangular chapel attached to a now derelict two storey house.

There is a graveyard in which the oldest apparent stone is from 1856 and the most conspicuous is the most recent, that of Professor John Griffiths, a cancer surgeon buried in 2001.

A wonderful doorstep at the most remote chapel in Wales (2019)

Photo taken during a visit to Soar y mynydd in 2019. The vacant dwelling is to the right and the chapel to the left

Simple and elegant Soar y mynydd chapel (2019)

Lewis's ears. Wendy, Beth and Kate rode out along the ancient drovers' route from the hostel during their rest day to see the chapel in 1999. The singing of hymns can be heard from the tops of the hills when the congregation are there

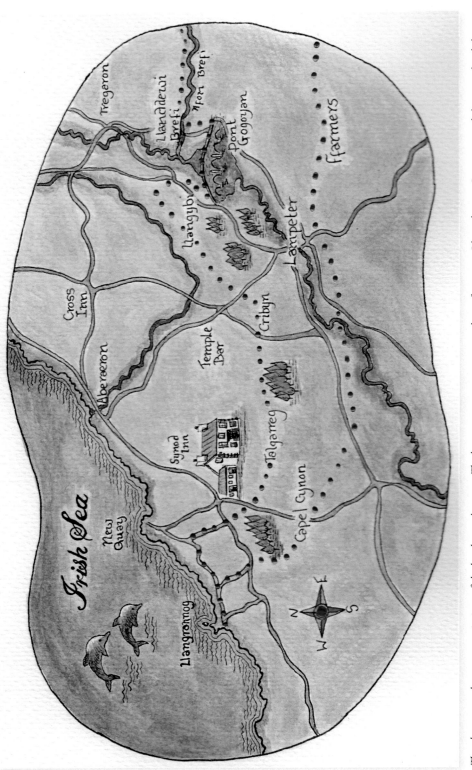

The above map shows two variations of the last leg to the coast. The horses were sometimes grazed at a farm near Llangybi near Lampeter and they completed the last stage on the following day.

CHAPTER 9

Eyes to the Irish Sea

Saddled up after a day of rest soaking up Elenydd tranquillity, we trotted off leaving the midges, towards the civilisation that is Llandewi Brefi.

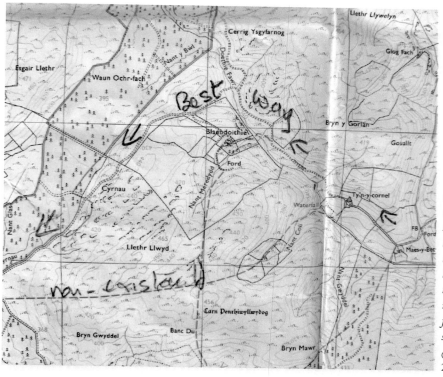

What a charming bridleway marked on the map, straight from the hostel doorstep, through what looks like the tumble-down remains of a farmstead or shepherd's hut.

© Ordnance Survey 2021

We could argue that the above bridleway does "exist" but totally impassable due to bogs and vegetation. Oh well, not far around the lane at least.

How different this area would look if it is planted with the proposed 36 x 480ft high turbines across the valley at Nant y Rast. How would the red kites survive amongst those? Wind power though renewable still comes at a price.

Having written off the bridleway opposite the hostel, we would briefly join the main Llandewi Brefi herd drovers' route. They of course would have been driving the beasts in the opposite direction, always towards England to fatten and sell. Their route went via Cwm Dulas, a house believed to be the site of an old tavern used in the 1840's and situated about half way between Llandewi Brefi and Ty' n Cornel.

The drovers' would have headed on to Blaendoethie (head of the Doethie) and Ty' n Cornel, maybe they too would have taken rest amongst the midges whose descendants found us so delicious. The drovers would have crossed the hills to Soar y mynydd and on to Abergwesyn. Needless to say a descent of Doethie valley would have resulted in far too many animals being lost over the cliffs with the pushing and shoving of a herd.

For the trekkers the silent little lane to Llandewi Brefi could feel never-ending, ambling along the tarmac through conifers that all looked the same. Emma remembers somewhere in those quiet woods nearly breaking down with despair that Polly and Rosie had now been singing the same Wham song continually for two whole days. "We

The girls and horses riding away from Ty'n Cornel along the ancient drovers' route in 1998. Nicola remembers taking a moonlit walk to this bridge one night to escape the snoring in the hostel.

used to like that song!" she ruefully reminded me recently, "until Polly and Rosie ruined it!" So to the sound of Wham we plodded on towards Llandewi Brefi.

Polly with her musical talents also formed a Soprano duet with Catherine one year and they both sang out loud their own "Cocoa Lotion" rendition of Kylie's version of "Locomotion".

They weren't the only accounts of our musical talents. Nicola and Alex remember singing "I Will Survive" by Gloria Gaynor at full volume together upon their horses, on top of the world on their adventure. Something about the beautiful wilderness of the Elenydd inspired our riders to sing their hearts out.

We visited Llandewi Brefi in 2019 and got absolutely soaked to the skin as the heavens opened as we left the car. A group of ladies smiled and chatted beneath a windswept canopy, raising money for their church, whilst torrents of rainwater channelled past their slip-on shoes. They were selling cakes, scotch eggs and quiches and we took some to eat on our way across the mountain road. My daughter and I were offered the use of a neighbour's toilet and the shop keeper was friendly and helpful. We were only there for half an hour but left with the feeling that the place had a most endearing community spirit.

Llandewi Brefi on a rainy day in 2019. The town became famous after being used as a location in the comedy "Little Britain", where Myfanwy and Dafydd lived.

The counties of Wales are rather complex, with historic counties, preserved counties, unitary authorities and principal areas. During the 80's and early 90's we rode through the English county of Shropshire and into Wales where we traversed Powys and Dyfed. After 1996, the counties we rode across took a different format. Shropshire, Powys, Carmarthenshire (just the north eastern tip of the county at Rhandirmwyn) then into Ceredigion, as it remains today. Rhandirmwyn and Llandewi Brefi were once both in Dyfed. Today they are both in separate original counties that existed prior to the creation of Dyfed in 1974. The only difference being, what was previously called Cardiganshire is now called Ceredigion.

So at the time of writing, the next spectacular landmark on our odyssey can be found in the county of Ceredigion.

This is a beautiful Grade II listed single-track stone bridge over the waters of the Teifi known as Pont Gogoyan. Pont being the Welsh word for bridge.

It became a tradition whereby the horses would cool down here, wade and drink and we would eat our picnic having met up with our Land Rover crew.

Crossing Pont Gogoyan in 1990 (Photo courtesy of David Elliott)

Myself on Maz, Judy on Shally, Matthew on Tenpee, Rosie on Camille, Louise on Shammy and Bossy Boot's nose 1990 (Photo courtesy of David Elliott)

Zac cools down with Charlie 2000

Charlie on Harvey and Rach on Mandela, who would always paw the water to make a splash! 1998

Nicola on Jack, Wendy on Lewis, Kate on Gilly, Beth on Hercules and Mandela's nose far left 1999

1990 was a particularly hot year. The horses gratefully drink from the river Teifi. Louise on Bossy Boots, Sue on Charlotte, myself on Maz, Chris on Lizzy, Catherine on Sherbie, Judy on Shally, Edward on Tenpee and Abi on Tango. Carrots was having a shoe replaced elsewhere! (Photo courtesy of Jane Osgathorp)

All smiles from Jane as she and Ruth let Bosun and Casper cool down in 1991 (Photo courtesy of Jane Osgathorp)

The final day's ride was mostly farmland, tracks and country lanes. There were a multitude of gates to be opened and closed and progress was often slow on what was already a long day, with many miles to be covered. Spirits were high none the less and although there were disputes over the existence of bridleways there was also much fun to be had. Rachael and the girls found it hilarious charging across the fields only to hear the shouts ring back along the string of horses: "Gate!" followed by "Pile up!". It was much like the grand national when a horse falls at a fence and a consortium of riders and horses end up in a tangled mess or maybe more akin to the Thelwell cartoons.

Farmers frequently tried to stop us from using the bridleways that passed through their land on this final day. If we managed to stick to our route it was a long 36 mile haul over the headland. It was as if a final frontier had to be conquered before we were to reach our sandy destination, there were many encounters with furious landowners.

On one such encounter, there was much shouting and Ruth was sent to the nearest house to call the police. She recalls her terror when she was shocked by an electric fence on her way. Stunned and bewildered and probably only about 10 years old.

Similarly I recall finding an electric fence across a bridleway, and whilst I tried to undo it, my dear Maz became entangled in it and careered around the field with the live fence zapping him as it trailed from his body. The image still haunts me.

One Dyfed landowner in particular caused us much strife. On several occasions he tried to stop us, not just from passing, but also from leaving his land, held hostage under some twisted irony whereby the alleged "trespasser" became the incarcerated. He used to position a crow scarer close to the bridleway, setting of shots every couple of minutes, and I don't for a second believe its purpose was to deter crows.

Nicola mentioned to me how they tried to ride as quietly as they could along that bridleway and it was always the very last gate that was blocked. At which point they did whatever they could to find an alternative escape route as quickly possible.

Kylee recalls riding through the place in question and being told by the adults to "Gallop like hell!" They also reminded her that "One farmer once threatened us with a gun!" Field after field they successfully ticked off, until the final track revealed a huge mechanical roller blocking the gate and spanning hedge to hedge. The sinking feeling in all those tired tummies must have been overwhelming at the thought of turning around and facing the possible consequences of an incredibly irate human being. The farmer caught up with them and they became trapped.

Joyce was once sent on foot to get help and had to climb over a fence and ask the first person she came upon to call the police. It happened to be the house of the farmhand whose wife opened the door. She was undoubtedly expected to side with her husband's wage provider and feeling very awkward proceeded to busy herself in the kitchen, whilst pointing to the phone in the hall and looking the other way.

Before long a male and female officer arrived and tried to calm the farmer down. In the end one officer offered a distraction whilst the other helped the riders escape discreetly through a neighbouring gate. From this point onwards it was agreed the police would meet us at the point of issue each year to escort us and the horses through. I wonder why Judy chose to keep using that path? Because "It is a right of way!'? No, we continued to use it because it meant the horses and riders avoided a stretch of busy A-class road streaming with caravans, motorhomes, motor bikes and lorries. I suppose if you had to choose between a 10-tonne lorry travelling at 40 mph or a red faced farmer with his knickers in a twist, then our reasons may be better understood.

The premise of being faced with that hostility on our first day trekking home four weeks later didn't seem to ruin anybody's holiday. By all accounts Judy once tried a different tactic in order to get her little herd through the bridleway.

Poor Ursula had been trying to encourage Zac into the sea on his very first seaside holiday and a wave washed over his back causing him to panic, spin around and trample on Ursula's thigh. A whopper of a bruise was pulsating under her jodhpurs as they left the coast and headed back for Ty' n Cornel. She wasn't able to rise to the trot, therefore the paces were either walk, canter or gallop.

Again, at the same farm, they became subject of the farmer's capture, but this time, tired of whipping the farmers or getting them arrested, Judy pleaded "But she's injured!" pointing to Ursula. "You must let us through, she has an awful injury. Pull your pants down and show him Ursula!!". A request which Ursula refused and turned scarlet and the farmer also turned scarlet, this time from embarrassment not fury, and quickly waved them all through.

One lady resident who lived on a bridleway route close to the coast used to run outside screaming at the riders when she heard the horses' hooves. Sometimes a tired and thirsty horse would try to drink from an overflowing rain water barrel on the path and she would shout and scream and order that we pay her money for the water.

Judy's account of the 1989 trek continues. Riding all the way from Bryn Poeth that year it would have been a very long ride and luckily the shoe was cast nearer civilisation and not in the middle of the Epynt somewhere…

> *"Lost a shoe! Miracle! Found a blacksmith. Camaes Evans, lovely guy, quite fancied you myself but your eyes were on the girls. Don't blame you though, they are lovely and they know it. So the four adults went on ahead that day. My turn to drive again – only fair as I am the only one trekking all the way home as well. Waited with the four girls while the shoeing was done. They set off about 1 o'clock with Emily map reading plus memory. Quite a tricky route that day, being a cross-country route with continual left or right turns – only about four miles of bridleways and many miles of lanes. They did well and did not go wrong once."*

The Dyfed headland before we reached the shores of the Irish sea was a tangle of lanes with a few bridleways. It was a long day in the saddle, our limbs were sore yet our spirits were high as we rode down the bumpy farm road to Penralt, where the horses were to stay.

I always remember the farm as a place of cheerful chaos. There were animals and people everywhere. Horses, cats, numerous different types of dogs and the pot-bellied pig of course. After the final unsaddling, the horses would roll and settle down to graze.

A typical bridleway on the final days riding on the Dyfed coastal headlands. Stopping for a rest in 1988. Emma and I sit on the bank. Janie, Bronwen, Gemma, Sandy and Filly relax before the final push to the sea. (Photo courtesy of Jack Upsall)

Judy's account of our arrival in Llangrannog in her 1989 manuscript captures the essence of our euphoria:

> "The first group arrived at Penralt, Llangrannog at around 3 o'clock and my girls came in about 7 o'clock (after the farrier replaced a shoe). The horses were turned out in a field below the farm with plenty of grass and a stream.
>
> The next evening we took them down to the beach. Janie is the bravest in the sea, like her mother before her. This is her third holiday by the sea and once she is over the initial shock of the cold water, she swims around amongst the boats with Rosie or Polly on board, ears pricked, surging up and down like a huge sea animal. Rosie says it's better than any fairground roundabout! The others were more cautious but after two weeks Shally did a few swimming strokes with me beside him

and became used to the waves breaking over his back.

On that last eight miles on the final day of the trek, when you come up over the hill and take your first glimpse of the sea from your horse whom you have ridden 120 miles from Shropshire, you get a wonderful tingly feeling of achievement. But that next evening when you find yourself and your horse in the water on Llangrannog beach, you feel and you know that your dream 'to ride to the sea' has come true."

I was certainly always dizzy with excitement as we dropped down through the woods. Carpeted with Harts-Tongue ferns and ivy. Old stone walls cloaked in mossy foliage. Past the old barns, now a beautifully converted home with a glass gable end. We would run down onto the tiny tarmacked road to join the Llangrannog road, past the church, the waterfall, ducking to the left down the teeny tiny road where the buildings get swiped with colour from the paint of the cars with over-ambitious drivers. Past the beautiful big painting of the ship on the side of The Ship Inn (heart-breaking that somebody since

painted over it!) to the beach, the sand between our toes. Seagulls, chips, beach fires and cider. A full four weeks of fun to be had.

The wonderful painting that used to be on the gable end of the Ship Inn, Llangrannog

CHAPTER 10

Llangrannog

Our destination, Llangrannog. Taken whilst standing next to the statue of St Caranog on the southern cliff top (2019)

After much excitement, having finally arrived at the coast, Judy stayed for four weeks before trekking home again. Many other trekkers just did the outward journey, others did the homeward journey, and a few did both. Most of the riders however got the opportunity to introduce their horses to the sea.

The descendants of Chalice were real sea-horses; Tina, Lassie, Janie and Mandela all swam in the deep sea waters.

Nicola and Mandela in the Irish Sea 1998

Nicola and Mandela 1998

Gentle encouragement in 1988. Myself on Sandy, Polly on Filly, Catherine on Bronwyn, Muff on Kasia and Judy with Janie (Photo coutesy of Jack Upsall)

And the sea horses are in! 1988 (Photo courtesy of Jack Upsall)

Karen and myself with Beau and Mandela in the waves in front of Carreg Bica, the rock that stands between Llangrannog and Cilborth beaches (2000). According to legend, this stack of Ordovician rock on the beach is the tooth of the giant Bica. He lived in Ceredigion and was forced to spit his tooth onto the beach when suffering a bad toothache.

Some needed more encouragement that others! Above is Mooney, a beautiful Highland mare with amazing natural highlights in her mane. She was owned by Karen and she eventually went out with the big boys in the waves, but it took a few days (2000)

Emma and I once boxed our ponies down to Llangrannog in the Autumn of 1988. What cheats! We had a lot of fun on the empty beaches with Sandy and Brandy though.

Edward on Tenpee, Abigail on Tango and Louise riding Bossy Boots in 1990 (Photo courtesy of David Elliott)

Nicola cantering Jack across the sand. Sometimes we rode the horses to Penbryn beach which offered the horses a lot more space and a long beach to gallop along.

Sue tries to encourage Sherbie to step into the water with Abigail and Tango behind in 1990 (Photo courtesy of David Elliott)

Nicola with Jack. It's difficult to imagine by looking at him with Nicola in this photo that he was a rescue horse. Once confined in a crate as a stallion in Cheshire. He never liked to be on his own and preferred a hackamore rather than a bit in his mouth. Llangrannog beach, 1998

The village shop run by Pete and Jan and their family for years and years provided us with provisions and the collection of pubs and restaurants were a great treat. The local fisherman - Tyvian, would sell us fresh crab and lobster which we would painstakingly prepare for great feasts. Learning all about the dead man's fingers in the process. The teens would walk up to the Gilfach caravan park to meet other holiday makers and get up to mischief at the bars. Friends would come and stay with us for a while then they would go and others would come. It was a wonderful way to spent the summer holidays to a child raised in a landlocked yet beautiful county, far away.

As you may imagine the incidents continued, only now there tended to be a larger audience comprising of the holiday makers visiting the town. We soon learned to take the horses onto the beach in the evenings so as not to upset other people enjoying the sand, sun and surf. Even so, you cannot please everybody all of the time.

Robbie recalls how delighted Barry felt that his Celia, James and the ladies had ridden all the way from Shropshire. He proudly watched as the girls all scampered down the beach, apparently in bra and knickers upon their horses, to swim with them in the sea. He explained in wonder their achievement to another father on the beach "They've ridden all the way from Shropshire you know!" The father curtly replied "Lovely! How wonderful. I've brought my kids to the beach for the day and now it's covered in horse crap!"

The novelty and excitement of the horses on the sands even inspired our Barry to have a ride. Maybe he imagined galloping under the sunset, like a horse whisperer at one with his steed. In reality Joyce and Celia had to carefully ride each side of Barry and "hold him on". Photographs are great for reliving memories and it's a shame we don't have one for this scene although imagination can do wonders.

James recalls riding Velvet on the beach. "I remember cantering bareback down the beach on a wet and slimy horse, trying to stay on. Finally the Fell pony started galloping and then I realised why. You and your friends came flying up behind us on your Thoroughbreds and Arabs. It was quite a sight watching the Thoroughbreds gracefully flying through the air with little effort and the red Arabs colours lit up by the setting sun, tails in the air like a flag"

James trying to convince Velvet to go in the sea. Shortly after he jumped on and Judy led them in, just deep enough for Velvet's back to get slimy and slippery before the 'bombing off across the beach bareback' took place. Polly is riding Janie in the background (1989)

There was fun to be had on Llangrannog beach for the canines too. It wasn't just the equines and humans who enjoyed the ambience of the seaside town.

Judy was deliberately looking the other way one busy afternoon on the beach in the summer of 89, when my golden retriever, Sadie, was approached by Tyson from The Ship Inn. Tyson was also a purebred golden retriever, a fine specimen and unusually dark in colour, a pleasant change from all the platinum retrievers that seemed to be popular at that time. Before Judy could intervene, which had never been her intention, the dogs proceeded to "join forces". Various onlookers pointed and commented as Judy gazed away up the beach. All was going marvellously until Kenchi shouted "Mum!! Look! The dogs! What is Sadie doing with that dog?! They are stuck mum!".

So Sadie's daughter Holly was conceived in front of all the holiday makers. After a quick conversation with Dee and Kevin from the Ship, they dug out Tyson's very respectable pedigree and on Sadie's delivery of a beautiful litter of pups, Tyson Of Crannog had earned a respectable stud fee. Holly was born in October and also ran to Llangrannog across the Welsh mountains with the horses many times, as did her daughter Cassie. So we now had a foal and a litter of puppies as a result of some rather frisky Welsh animals.

Our golden retrievers were an integral part of the treks for many years. Above to the left is Holly, conceived on Llangrannog beach, daughter of Affcot Sadie and Tyson of Crannog. Next to Holly is Cassie, her daughter. Alison remembers Judy once pointing to somebody's house where a golden retriever could be seen coming out of a kitchen "Look at that! A dog just like Holly!" Judy laughed. Needless to say it was Holly (1999)

The seaside village of Llangrannog was established around its church during the 6th century. There is also evidence of an earlier settlement at nearby Dinas Lochtyn, which dominates the local landscape. The sea has always been the most important element in the development of the village and dominated the lives of its inhabitants.

Between 500 and 548 AD Saint Carantoc established a religious settlement not far from the seashore. He was a sea traveller and leader of a small band of saints that brought Christianity to the western seaboard. The church built on St Carantoc's sacred enclosure acted as a nucleus around which a few houses were built. The small "Church Village" was never visible from the sea due to narrow twists of the Hawen river and therefore never a temptation for marauders that once infested the Ceredigion coast.

Until the seventeenth century the village of Llangrannog remained a tiny hamlet. Ffynnonfair (St Mary's holy well), provided not only drinking water but also medicinal water that could cure all ills.

It wasn't until well into the 18th century that Llangrannog became a port. By 1750 seafaring had become an established occupation.

This "Beach Village" continued to developed and the two villages eventually joined together. Culm, lime and general merchandise were imported and exports included salted butter, preserved herrings and Cardigan bricks. Ships were built in Llangrannog between the years of 1787 and 1859. During the twentieth century tourism replaced seafaring as the principal activity of the village.

Today it is a great attraction for summer visitors but remains unspoilt possibly due to the limited parking available in the village.

On a fine day we would pack a picnic and head to the peninsula known as Ynys Lochtyn, sometimes during low tide Judith would swim from beach to beach, to the island. Those beaches were only accessible by sea. We would watch dolphins and seals, explore secret beaches and loll around on the grass in the summer sun.

There is a legend that a giant called Bica, who lived in Ceredigion, had a raging toothache. As he stamped about in pain, the tremendous noise disturbed a dwarf called Lochtyn, who advised him to go to the coast, where his tooth would fall out. In return for his advice, the dwarf wanted a small island where he could live quietly by himself. The giant set off and as he reached the coast, one of his footsteps created Llangrannog beach and his tooth fell out, creating Carreg Bica. He reached out his finger and drew it across a rocky peninsula, separating off a tiny island for the dwarf Ynys Lochtyn.

Judy and Tim sit with Holly on the un-grazed island called Ynys Lochtyn in 1993. Often dolphins can be seen from this peninsula

Joyce and Tim with Holly in 1993 relaxing on Ynys Lochtyn. It was a climb to get across to this tussocky island which is characterised by a streak of white quartz.

Charlie plays with Cassie in the long grass on Ynys Lochtyn

Standing on the peninsula looking back to where the Iron Age hill fort once stood. Traeth yr ynys, the small beach in the picture, can be accessed via a steep narrow track and a scramble at the bottom. The sea this side of the peninsula is often calm like a mill pond (2019)

Sunsets at Llangrannog are breath-taking 2013 (Photo courtesy of Israel Archuletta)

Steep steps on the coastal path between Llangrannog and Penbryn, not suitable for hooves!

Taking the southerly coastal path from Llangrannog brings yet more wondrous examples of nature. After a mile or so of steep ups and downs a beach and Carreg y Ty, meaning "Rock House", are accessed via a narrow path. A 20 foot rock face must be scrambled down to enjoy this gem and it often only has a handful of agile visitors each day, remaining beautifully unspoilt.

Underneath the grass covered rock is a cave which has a ghostly feeling to it. The sound of the waves crashing within the depths of the cavern resonate like a bellowing monster and both children and dogs run away from its mouth, too afraid to enter.

*A Willow Herb
meadow frames the
beach and Carreg
y Ty (Rock House)
which becomes an
island when the
tide rises. There is
a small cliff face to
negotiate to spend
time on this beach
(2014)*

*The spooky cave
under Carreg y Ty,
The Rock House
(2019)*

The coastal path continues through all the little coastal towns and villages into south Wales. Penbryn is one such beach we used to ride to, via the country lanes, to let the horses really stretch their legs, the sands here being much longer than at Llangrannog.

A link between Shropshire and Llangrannog was forged over the years and some Llangrannog families started to join the treks. Wendy, Beth and Kate Brice trekked with Judy on the eastward return for a couple of years and stayed at Affcot Mill, exploring beautiful local Shropshire bridleways before boxing their horses back home to the coast. Alison, Rachael and Emma Kinsey with a friend, Cherry, are another Llangrannog family who brought their horses to Shropshire then trekked westerly back home on our outward journey.

The first day riding home was an experience for Charlotte Bell one year as she'd not spent more than an hour or two in the saddle prior to it. By all accounts she was white as a sheet when she arrived at Ty n Cornel. Her mother Steph knew she'd have been too shy to say anything such as "Could we slow down please?". Charlotte however came on many treks afterwards, becoming one of the long timers, so she hadn't been put off. She also became very involved in the Endurance scene afterwards, travelling to France to crew for Judy's horse who was part of the British Team.

The trek home in 1989 was interlaced with disaster and comedy. The first day in the saddle saw the riders getting hopelessly lost. They were only two miles from their stopover at Lampeter yet spent two hours going around in circles. Unfortunately the Tymons' horses had to be boxed back to their home in Llangrannog after developing a nasty cough.

The second day was the ride from Lampeter to Bryn Poeth and Sue and Ray Field had travelled up from the respectable town of Harpenden in Hertfordshire to support the riders which included daughter Ros. This not only involved driving a rickety old Land Rover but also staying at Bryn Poeth YHA. They were aghast at the primitive lifestyle that beheld them, with no vehicular access or electricity and where it was pouring with rain yet there was still no water coming from the taps.

Drama occurred when a suspected flasher was seen across the valley from the hostel. Bob, Ray and some other fellow hostellers sorted it out according to the trek journal that year. Then a different kind of drama unfolded when Fiona fell down the ladder-like stairs and broke her ankle! Of all the places for this to happen, Bryn Poeth Uchaf was the most inconvenient. Again with great chivalry, Bob, Ray and Ov carried her down the mountainside to the car where Ov took her to the casualty.

Then the dreaded cough swept through the herd and one by one the horses needed rescuing with the horsebox. By the second to last day Sue and Rijal were the only pair still going. Those horses who hadn't already been boxed home, were led on foot by their riders. Plenty of miles were completed by the riders on their own two feet during the summer of 1989.

And so the horses would settle back into their fields and stables, the riders would ease back into their home comforts. Some living in the beautiful county of Shropshire others from different parts of the country, several Londoners' took part in the treks over the years. People would go back to their jobs, universities, schools and home lives and tales would be told for years to come about the treks. Memories made, good and bad to be shared with future generations.

Here follows a little rhyme about our last trek to the sea led by Judith…

ODE TO TREK 2000

Karen and Jenny, Mooney and Beau
Quite unaware of the distance to go.
Zac and Mandela, done it before
Trace, Em and Charlie all knew the score!
For Judy and Holly the umpteenth time
But Kizzy in a hen-house?
That bumped her pride!
Also the mountain bike, "Didn't IT do well?"
It didn't feel so willing up some sodding hills!

First to Clun, a nice gentle start,
From Kizzy a pheasant, from Holly a partridge,
Nice comfy beds and beer at The Sun,
Met the locals - the quiz was fun!

Next was to Bleddfa, to Margaret and Bob,
Three wolves, a foal and the rocking horse Cobweb,
With gorgeous food, beer and wine,
To Charlotte's side was Bob's bee-line!
Drunken voices send us to sleep,
Dreams of hunting and "When's the next meet?"
Off in the morning, did Margaret wince?
When two rotten birds were in place of her mince!

Next was to Rhulen, over the hills,
And again at Mike's our glasses were filled.
What a perfect husband to cope with us lot,
Kids, pigs and chickens and casserole pot!
The breakfast was lovely, there was no lie-in,
The cockerel knew when we were to begin.

So now to Llanwrtyd, across the hills,
Where we thought our Karen had popped Beau some pills,
The 'Fire Breathing Dragon' with Tracey on top,
Saw the finishing line at Ascot!

The Neuadd Arms where the dragon dwells,
Curries, beers and attic smells,
Nice mountain bikers and bog swimming games,
Birds nest in your bedroom
A little deranged!
Some beers and the TV, how simply ideal.
"What?!" Gasps Tracey. "No Ally Mcbeal?!"

Next to the hostel at Ty'n Cornel,
From the heights of the mountains, you hear Mooney's bell.
To the depths of the valley you can see Zac's spots,
Holly and Kizzy are just tiny dots.

Up the side of a mountain the Land Rover rocks,
A pale-looking Judy just trying not to stop!
And at last to the hostel a beautiful place,
Where a figure eagerly waits at the gate.
Roger the warden, a bit of crier,
"Easy with the gas! Don't touch the fire!"
Useful and helpful, yet can't read a map
Could have been worse, a tolerant chap.

Nice food from Judy, I'd almost forgot,
How a Spag Bolognese could be so bloody hot!
And poor Mrs Williams at this peaceful place,
Where our harmonious snores drove her red in the face!
And one by one they left the dorm,
To wake on a table to greet the morn,

And so our last day, the longest of all.
My poor, poor legs felt so bloody sore.
Jenny on bike given so many gates.
Keep open the chippy! We might be late!
How many maps have we still to go through?
Oh! That's not so bad, only the two!

And so we arrived , Llangrannog coast,
A beer, some food and all birds to roost.
The horses all grazing under the trees,
Quite unaware of what morning will see.
The walk down the hill after such a long haul,
To the biggest and scariest puddle of all!

Mandela and Beau in the sea straight away,
Zac on the lead, having a play.
The bays in their element swimming around,
Charlie and Karen, screaming out loud!
Mooney at last persuaded to go
Out with the big boys with Emily in tow.
Jenny on Zac, all of them in,
"Just watch out for the children having a swim!"

Our trek 2000
Off to the sea!
Girlies and horses
What more do you need?!

EMILY COLLYER 2000

A NOTE IN MEMORY OF MY FATHER, EDWARD

Dad was the least horsey person you could imagine but incredibly tolerant as was his nature in general. He built stables and fences, took photographs at pony club and supported mother's hobby without question. He even led dear Witty down the lane on his final day, feeding him grass before he was put to sleep. Dad was a legend and we all still miss him. He died at the grand age of 100 years in 2011.

He was never involved in the treks and I never even saw him on a horse. He used to joke about when he rode once as a youngster, the horse in front of him farted each time its rider sat to the rising trot. He was an incredibly intelligent man and a director of housing in government. He also had a wicked sense of humour, often toilet humour in which I most definitely share his amusement. He was the most kind, patient and loving father any child could wish for.

Dad was an artist. He exhibited paintings in the Royal Academy of Arts, including a piece that hung in Lord's cricket ground for many years. He preferred to paint life drawings, in oils especially. He mostly painted beautiful women, but on occasion men too. He was incredibly talented.

My father's life perhaps deserves a book in itself. I'm sure my siblings would agree, but for the purposes of this book I will include one of his pieces of art in which his humour has prevailed (note the naked man showing off his catch). I think Dad would approve.

Edward presumably had his own vision of our treks to the sea! Painting by Edward Charles Collyer (1989)

AFTERWORD

Writing about these journeys has been a journey in itself. I have rediscovered places and events from my childhood and adolescence that I had forgotten. Mid Wales is vast and beautiful and its essence became so embedded in my childhood that it closely competes with South Shropshire in my memories and recollections.

I long to go back and explore mid Wales again and again. The towns and villages are litter free, MacDonald's free, commercially unruined and each village feels unique.

It's been humbling. Whilst setting out to tell our tales I've been drawn into bigger, darker and deeper tales; things that happened along the way in history that I can barely fathom. It's become a journey through time whereby I'm just a wayfarer in a mere snippet of time, though we added to history in our own little way - history that is massive, vast, complicated, at times devastating yet so very important to identities, the present and the future lying ahead of us.

I have travelled by railway, bicycle, car and on foot, ironically all but on horseback, to attempt to piece together and locate where a sprawled and tangled scattering of memories were once born, whilst leaving others resting in their mysterious past.

It strikes me how unusual such an unravelling will have become as everything is now documented on social media or simply time-lined by photos on our phones. I therefore feel privileged to have been able to put my heart and soul into this book.

Various childhood memories and images have clicked into place as I've made this literary journey. Other memories and visions of places may well remain "somewhere in Wales" at least for now.

Many places along the route I now see in a completely different light due to the local history I have discovered. It is like I have trekked the route again only this time looking around me on a deeper level. Once more I have absorbed into my being nature's true wonder and the sheer beauty of the hills, but in addition I have considered the lives of the people along the way, both in the past and present.

Will a friend or descendant of one of the trekkers one day repeat the adventure? Will somebody stumble upon this book and wish to rediscover the once regular route. Twenty one years later in this digital era it could be quite a different story. Digital mapping, instant photography, the flexibility of Air B&B and the improvement of rights of way may facilitate the adventure.

However when the signal goes down and the battery dies… you'd be on a wild Welsh mountain, just as we were, hoping you take the right route across a deep black bog.

I hope you have enjoyed the book and here follows some appendices containing more information about the treks.

Emily, 2019

Appendix 1

The People

Riders and Drivers

Judy, Paul, Oliver, Emily and Rosie Collyer
Kenchi McCann (Collyer)
Chris, Morris, Nick and Andy Haynes
Belinda Critchley (Haynes)
Joyce, Rob and Tim Machin
Tania Hughes (Machin)
Kerry Baskerville (Machin)
Joan and Sam Hay
Sue and Bob Trueman
Beck Burton (Trueman)
Celia, Barry and James Russell
Sue and Ross Nickless
Lucy Nickless Callwood
Ruth Morris (Nickless)
Andy Nickless
Polly Sampson (Earnshaw)
Damon Earnshaw
Emma Holden Ostle
Stephanie and Charlotte Bell
Alison and Steve Hall
Alison Gill (Moore)
Alexandra Nicholls
Gayle Routledge
Jack and Ruth Upsall
Catherine Richmond (Upsall)

Vivien Wheeler

Jane Osgathorp

Nicola Young

Tracey Pearson

Jenny Slawson

Karen Harwood

Joanna Chick (Wrench)

Ursula Hargreaves

Wendy and Beth Brice

Kate Reed (Brice)

Sue and Ray Field

Ros Hales (Field)

Anne Platts

Julia Collings

Mary Massey

Alison and Emma Kinsey

Rachel Bailey (Kinsey)

Cherry Brookin

Sue Gent

Edward, Matthew and Joseph Evans

Barry Evans

Abigail Horobin (Evans)

Louise Pearn (Powell)

Chris, David and Matthew Elliot

Catherine Pound (Elliot)

Hilary Condron

Kylee Williams

Helen Smart

Jan Pritchard

Margaret and Bob Gardiner

Jean, Celia and Tobin Tymons

The Herd

The following horses and ponies were part of the treks to the Welsh coast from Shropshire. Some only did sections, many did the whole journey and also the return trip.

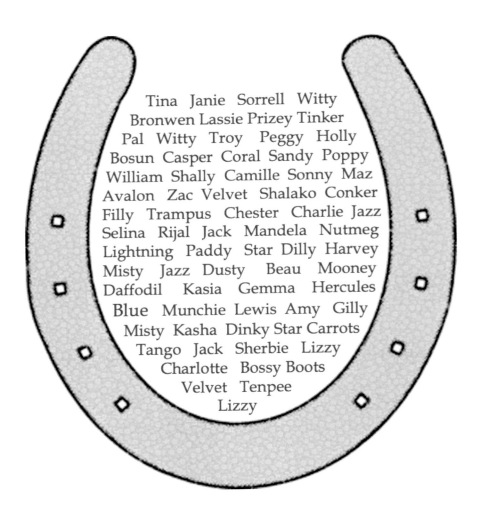

Tina Janie Sorrell Witty
Bronwen Lassie Prizey Tinker
Pal Witty Troy Peggy Holly
Bosun Casper Coral Sandy Poppy
William Shally Camille Sonny Maz
Avalon Zac Velvet Shalako Conker
Filly Trampus Chester Charlie Jazz
Selina Rijal Jack Mandela Nutmeg
Lightning Paddy Star Dilly Harvey
Misty Jazz Dusty Beau Mooney
Daffodil Kasia Gemma Hercules
Blue Munchie Lewis Amy Gilly
Misty Kasha Dinky Star Carrots
Tango Jack Sherbie Lizzy
Charlotte Bossy Boots
Velvet Tenpee
Lizzy

The Horse Family Tree

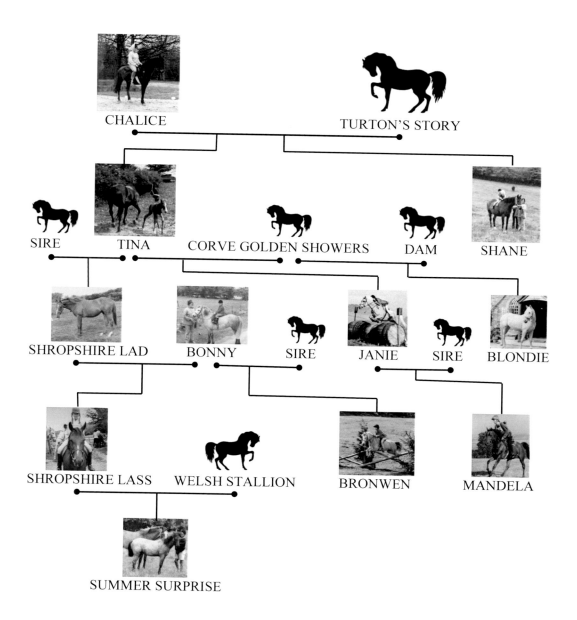

The Pack

THREE GENERATIONS OF GOLDEN RETRIEVERS

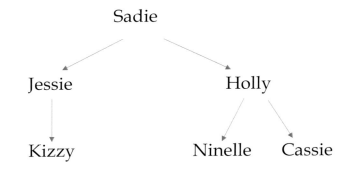

Sadie

Jessie — Holly

Kizzy

Ninelle — Cassie

Sometimes the dogs got tired and needed a lift!

APPENDIX 5

The Wheels

EHM 604J Series II Land Rover 1970

Often seen towing an extra-long horse trailer, that conveyed up to five ponies, to pony club rallies from 1978 up until 1985. Angus rode home in the back of this Land Rover in Jan 1979. Pooping down Judy's collar as she drove. Fitted with after-market side windows to give the pack of kids in the back some light and a view. Also fitted with some front spot lights. EHM didn't get to play "back up" on a sea-trek as naively we carried all our gear in saddlebags. Winner of all things pony club.

EHM 604J Series II Land Rover at a Pony Club rally 1985

YKV 409K Series III Land Rover 1971

Took over the Pony Club duties from around 1986 in addition to Endurance competitions. Last sea-trek was 1990 aged 19. YKV blew up at Knighton in the Spring and must have been given one last repair as it was seen in Llangrannog in the summer. YKV wins the Veteran category. Seen on the right in the picture below on its last season.

YKV 409K Series III Land Rover at the campsite in Llangrannog, 1990

D768 OOP Land Rover Defender 1986.

First sea-trek was 1991. Numerous Endurance competition duties. Last sea-trek 1998 aged 12. Backed us up for 8 sea-treks. D'OOP is the clear winner in this respect. Worst performer when it came to brakes and gears though.

D'OOP provides a picnic table before the riders crossed the firing range near Fron Farm in 1993

R759 AUX LAND ROVER DISCOVERY 1997

Last sea-trek 2000. Many trips around the country to Endurance competitions. Also impressive European heatmap including Norway, Switzerland and Compiegne in France. Passed on for retirement in 2017. R'AUX wins the "most travelled" category.

R'AUX was often seen with moss and seedlings growing from its window sills. Regularly stuffed with hay, straw and animal food just like its predecessors.

RANGE ROVERS

Range Rovers 1ˢᵗ Generation. With one in Tuscan Blue and one in Bahama Gold, they were an integral part of the sea-trek in 1990. Both made it off-road up to Bryn Poeth Uchaf youth hostel.

The Bahama Gold Range Rover at the firing range border (photo David Elliott 1990)

The Tuscan Blue Range Rover at Fron Farm picnic spot. (Photo David Elliott 1990)

There were likely other 4x4's and cars involved in the treks over the years including Robbie's Daihatsu which got diverted on the Hay-on-Wye trek in 1990 to a business meeting in London, leaving a rider-less horse.

Another set of wheels took the form of a cumbersome Westcoat mountain bike and was ridden mostly by Jenny, Tracey and myself in the 2000 trek. A heavy bike with no suspension. A right pain in the ass. Bikes and horses clearly don't go well together. Horses gallop uphill and walk down. Bikes speed downhill and crawl up. This results in the person with the route knowledge having a definite advantage. I understand Jenny's irritation at not only having to struggle with the bike but also being expected to open and close gates for those upon the horses. Sat on their high-horses like royalty!

Some kids bikes were also ridden in 1990 trek. According to David's journal the riders also had a tough time, through nettles especially.

Route Information

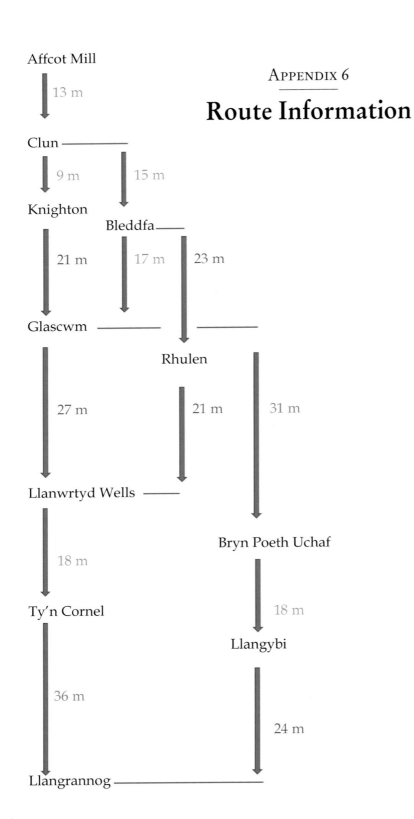

Affcot Mill

↓ 13 m

Clun

↓ 9 m   ↓ 15 m

Knighton

Bleddfa

↓ 21 m   ↓ 17 m   ↓ 23 m

Glascwm

Rhulen

↓ 27 m   ↓ 21 m   ↓ 31 m

Llanwrtyd Wells

↓ 18 m

Bryn Poeth Uchaf

Ty'n Cornel

↓ 18 m

Llangybi

↓ 36 m

↓ 24 m

Llangrannog

The following elevation profile is approximate and reflects the final route used.

The highest point in the route was near to the summit of Great Rhos in the Radnor Forest where we reached 1784 ft above sea level. The lowest point, other than the last drop to Llangrannog was the crossing of the river Wye at Erwood where we dropped to 370 ft above sea level.

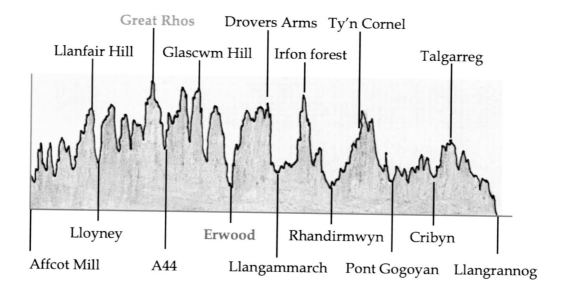

Total ascent - 18130 feet / 5526 metres

Total distance – 126 miles / 203 kilometres

Halfway point approx. Cwm Owen / The Griffin, Epynt

All distances are approximate and do not account for countless wrong turns taken over the years. GPS route information is available on request by email to cambriandreams@icloud.com

Two Fat Ladies

BY JUDY COLLYER (2006)

PART ONE – ARRIVAL

Welcome Ludworth Jemma to Shropshire. Jemma was born and raised in Ludworth, County Durham. She is a beautiful, shiny black Fell Pony, five years old. She has a mane and a tail that must weigh pounds and feathers long enough to put hair curlers in.

To say I have downgraded from Zak, my leopard spot Appaloosa/ TB/Arab endurance horse would be an insult to Jemma. Downsized is more the point, although I am not sure there is any less of her than

Zak. His rugs fit her, but she is nearer to the ground, stands still while I get on and off, and takes me up onto Wenlock Edge whenever I choose. Zak has gone to Cheshire for a new career in dressage and show jumping, he has settled in well.

Jemma's back accommodates my Western saddle – I won't ride in anything else. It was a matter of finding a horse to fit the saddle. She was a champion Fell pony in hand as a three year old. She is nicely put together with a beautiful, crested neck, bright kind eyes (when you draw the curtains of her forelock) and good movement. She is forward going and has a fast walk. Her education has included dressage and show jumping. In other words "a little gem" and a true-to-type Fell pony.

Guapo, Emily's Andalusian/TB is very pleased to have her here at Affcot Mill, having spent three weeks on his own when we took Zak to his new home. We're not quite sure which one is boss yet – I think they must have an understanding.

I have very stiff knees and found it increasingly difficult to get on and off Zak (15.3hh), sometimes having to walk home if I needed to get off for a gate or a pee. So my spirits have risen to heights not far short of Wenlock Edge these past weeks, when I have been pottering around on Jemma.

We hope to do some treks again next year, like we used to do before I became so involved in endurance competitions internationally with Ursula and Zak. Maybe we'll trek to the sea again (Llangrannog) but most certainly around Shropshire and possibly the Pennine Way – home ground to Jemma.

When Emily and I first saw a video of Jemma, we thought she was very fat. Even allowing for the fact that we are used to lean, muscly endurance horses, I was worried about laminitis. However, her hooves are fine and she's slimmed a bit since she's been here. But, like me, she is an "ample lady" and we both get puffed climbing up Wenlock Edge – me by vigorously kicking her and Jemma by carrying me up there! She is already noticeable fitter.

PART TWO – THE FOUR SEASONS ON WENLOCK EDGE

Unlike Vivaldi, I shall start with Autumn, because that is now…

TO AUTUMN

Season of Mist and mellow fruitfulness,
Close bosom-friend of the maturing sun;
Conspiring with him how to load and bless
With fruit the vines that round the thatch eaves run;
To bend with apples the mossed cottage-trees,
And fill all fruit with ripeness to the core;
To swell the gourd, and plump the hazel shells
With a sweet kernel; to set budding more,
And still more, later flowers for the bees,
Until they think warm days will ever cease,
For Summer has o'erbrimmed their clammy cells.

JOHN KEATS

Golden sunlight shining on reds, greens, browns, gold and yellows, creating an inflourescent glow on shimmering leaves.

We pause for a while, we smell the leaves, the fungi, the earth. Birds are still singing in this peaceful golden world and some little deer stand stock still for a moment, dappled amongst the trees, before scampering away when my dog appears, spooking a pheasant which noisily rises to the sky. We make our way through all these colours, sounds and smells to the picnic area near Westhope, and back round the lanes home.

WINTER

Whose woods these are I think I know
His house is in the village though;
He will not see me stopping here
To watch his woods fill up with snow.

We silently trot disturbing a covering of powdery snow, which muffles all sound. The inky black tree branches, silhouetted against the palest blue sky, seem sinister. We must not stand too long – darkness and cold will soon arrive. The thought of hay, rugs, tea and logs burning beckon us.

My little horse must think it queer
To stop without a farmhouse near
Between the woods and frozen lake
The darkest evening of the year.
He gives his harness bells a shake
To ask if there is some mistake
The only other sound's the sweep
Of easy wind and downy flake.

(FROM *STOPPING BY WOODS ON A SNOWY EVENING*
BY ROBERT FROST)

SPRING

Oh, to be in England
Now that April's there,
And whoever wakes in England
Sees, some morning, unaware,
That the lowest boughs and the brushwood sheaf
Round the elm-tree hole are in tiny leaf,
While the chaffinch sings on the orchard bough
In England – now!

(FROM *HOME – THOUGHTS FROM ABROAD*
BY ROBERT BROWNING)

Wood anemones, wild garlic, bluebells, buds bursting into sprays of tiny leaves, birds in chorus. Last years leaves amongst shooting plants and grasses.

So busy up here, like rush hour in the city, only cleaner.

How many springs has Wenlock Edge seen? I suspect little has changed since the last ice age.

> *Very old are the woods;*
> *And the buds that break*
> *Out of the brier's boughs,*
> *When March winds wake,*
> *So old with their beauty are-*
> *Oh, no man knows*
> *Through what wild centuries*
> *Roves back the rose.*
> *Very old are the brooks;*
> *And the hills that rise*
> *Where snow sleeps cold beneath*
> *The azure skies*
> *Sing such a history*
> *Of come and gone,*
> *Their every drop is as wise*
> *As Solomon.*

(*All That's Past* – Walter de la Mare)

Summer

> *Trees with the soot of August suns were black,*
> *Though splashed in places with a bright fire-light;*
> *I praised the daemon of that dim wood track*
> *Where pepper moths were flittering by night.*

(from *August* by A J Young)

The laden trees give cool shade, bees hum, dragon flies dart, butterflies flutter, rabbits scuttle. A hawk hovers, cows murmur lazily, a tractor drones in the distance, sheep and lambs fill the gaps.

But now we are going down to stand in the ford and cool ourselves.

If ever any of you are up on the southern end of Wenlock Edge in one of the four seasons, pause a while, look for a minute. You mind just see a dark shape amongst the trees relishing the precious place. It might just be us, Jemma and me – TWO FAT LADIES!

What a life, if full of care,
We have no time to stand and stare.
No time to stand beneath the boughs
And stare as long as sheep or cows.
No time to see, when woods we pass,
Where squirrels hide their nuts in grass.
No time to see, in broad daylight,
Streams full of stars, like skies at night.
No time to turn at Beauty's glance,
And watch her feet, how they can dance.
No time to wait till her mouth can
Enrich that smile her eyes began.
A poor life this if, full of care
We have no time to stand and stare.

(*Leisure* – WH Davies)

ACKNOWLEDGEMENTS

First and foremost my gratitude goes to my mother Judith, for providing me with such an adventurous childhood and the opportunity to put these experiences into a book. I've no doubt that the treks shaped the person I am today.

Thank you Marcus Field for you guidance and help throughout the whole project. For writing a fantastic foreword and back cover. Your patience with my endless questions was that of a saint. I would have been pretty lost without you!

I wish to thank all the trek participants and their families, riders and back up crew. Thank you for sharing your stories, memories and photographs with me for the purpose of this book and for helping to make our history. Much appreciation goes to all the people who responded to my persistent questions about the timeline whilst trying to distinguish between each trek.

A huge thank you for all the permissions to use the wonderful plethora of photographs discovered during the creation of this manuscript. Some excellent photography was displayed in a time well before digital photography was widespread. Especially thankyou to Nicola Young, Steph and Charlie Bell, Jack and Ruth Upsall, Jane Osgathorp, Nicola Young, Tracey Pearson, Jenny Slawson, Karen Harwood, Wendy Brice, Alison Kinsey, Chris and David Elliot. Please accept my apologies for not crediting each individual photo. It was sometimes unclear as to who owned the original photos.

To the horses, ponies and the dogs, I thank you from the bottom of my heart for being you. Loyal, trustworthy and therapeutic throughout our various worries and crisis.

Massive thanks to Jim for all your support, for your help with formatting, proof reading, general advice and child minding.

Thank you James Langton for proof reading on short notice.

Shelly, thank you for your design input.

To John Martin (YHA archivist), I thank you for your time and knowledge in the history of youth hostels and the access to your collection of fabric badges.

Andy Hazell sculptor, please accept my thanks for sharing information on what was once Knighton YHA

A special thank you to Carol Rogers for urging me to make this happen! For assuring me the stories would make a good book.

Archie and Minnie, thank you for accompanying me whilst re-treading parts of the route and letting me spend many hours researching and writing without distracting me too much!

Thank you Sue Truman for your help with some of the Welsh translation.

To Bob and Margaret Gardiner of Treboeth and all the other B&B hosts, I thank you for your fantastic hospitality, for riders, horses and dogs.

Thank you to Dorothy and Maurice Young who kindly let us stay in their holiday cottage in Clun during the later years of our trekking adventures.

To all the YHA hostel wardens, thank you for your patience and understanding with what must often have felt like a mass invasion to the peace and tranquillity of your hostel.

Thank you to the Youth Hostel Association for providing wonderful affordable accommodation for travellers.

Thank you to Wendy and Adrian Brice and prior to them, thank you to Jean and Richard Tymons for warmly welcoming us to Llangrannog and providing rest and grazing for the horses over the years.

A special heartfelt thanks to the people of Llangrannog for welcoming us to their home town during the summer holidays. To the landlords and ladies that housed and fed us over the years and a special thanks to Pete and Jan who ran the village shop for many years.

Many thanks to all my friends and family who have supported and encouraged me in any way whilst writing this book. From proof reading and critique, to advice on printing and publishing.

If I've missed any person who rode or drove on the treks please accept my apologies and gratitude for your contributions.

Thank you to Biddles Books for all your help and advice and for producing the final book.

BIBLIOGRAPHY/REFERENCES

localdroversroads.co.uk

walesonline.co.uk

YHA Historical listing - calmview.bham.ac.uk

rhandirmwyn.net

andyhazell.co.uk

ft.com The Walk File : Hopesay

shropshirehistory.com

english-heritage.org.uk

historicengland.org.uk

localdroveroutes.co.uk

erwoodstation.com

cpre.org.uk

Llangrannog. Exploring the heritage of a coastal village -
    J Geraint Jenkins

Uprooted Communities Epynt – Herbert Hughes

abandonedcommunities.co.uk

llangammarchhistory.co.uk

welshruins.co.uk

Welsh Cattle Drovers – Richard Moore - Colyer

Drovers Roads of Wales – Fay Goodwin and ShirleyToulson

Jim Perrin – Hills of Wales

Jim Perrin – Travels With The Flea

Here Be Dragons: The Elenydd audax – Emily Chappell

glascwmcommunitycouncil.co.uk

britainexpress.com

Shropshire. A Shell Guide – Michael Moulder

Welsh Border. The Wirral to the Wye - Gavin Gibbons

It Happened in Shropshire - Bob Burrows

Offa's Dyke Path – John B Jones

Welsh Place-names and Their Meanings – Dewi Davies

walesonline.co.uk Remembering the Tragedy of Welsh
    Speaking Epynt

An Idler On The Shropshire Borders – Ida Gandy

A Shropshire Lad – A E Housman

wyeexlorer.co.uk

commons.wikimedia.org

fishingpassports.co.uk

visitshropshirehills.co.uk

Deaf and Different - Doreen Woodford